Michelle Dewberry shot to fame during the second series of *The Apprentice,* when her shrewd, no-nonsense style made her Sir Alan's employee of choice, over more flamboyant competitors. She has now set up Michelle Dewberry Ltd, a consultancy advising businesses and individuals on how to restructure their operations in a more profitable form. Michelle's special interest is in working with teenagers who feel they don't fit into the conventional paths of education and careers structure. She is connected with several charities, most notably the Women's Aid Federation, which works to end domestic violence. She lives in Clapham, London. Visit her website at www.michelledewberry.com

Mel Billowes, who worked with Michelle on her story, is a journalist with twenty years' experience as a reporter and producer for the BBC and independent television companies. She is now a full-time writer and lives in Essex with husband Paul and children Sam, Daisy and Freddy. www.mvagency.com.

Anything is Possible

MICHELLE DEWBERRY

with Mel Billowes

An Orion paperback

First published in Great Britain in 2007
by Orion
This paperback edition published in 2008
by Orion Books Ltd,
Orion House, 5 Upper St Martin's Lane,
London WC2H 9EA

An Hachette Livre UK company

1 3 5 7 9 10 8 6 4 2

Printed and bound in Great Britain
by Clays Ltd, St Ives plc

The Orion Publishing Group's policy is to use papers that
are natural, renewable and recyclable products and
made from wood grown in sustainable forests. The logging
and manufacturing processes are expected to conform to
the environmental regulations of the country of origin.

www.orionbooks.co.uk

Contents

Dedication

To my mum, Karl, Clair, Marc, Paul and my nanna.
I love you all so much and am so very proud to call
you my family.

To my big sister Fiona. You are a truly special person,
who I love and miss every day. I hope I'm doing you
proud, the way you did me.

X

Acknowledgements

My sincere thanks go to the people below:

Ken, Carl and Lynsey – welcome to the family and thanks for all your support.

Moira –the help and support you have given me this year has been truly amazing. You lifted me up from rock bottom when I really needed it.

My true friends – you know who you are! I love you all and sometimes you deserve medals for putting up with me.

Mel Billowes – you started as my ghost writer but have now become my friend.

The Orion team – your patience while I made my continual changes has been massively appreciated.

Previous employers – you recognised and believed in my potential and helped me to grow:

The St John team for starting it all off, Julie Wilkerson and Sir Alan Sugar.

And finally …

The man at the top of my street – I'm not sure if you will read this book but if you do, I just wanted to say thanks for making me laugh, every day.

My heart is pounding so hard I think it's going to burst out of my chest. My mind is racing. I can hardly breathe. I feel scared, happy, confused, elated, proud — the list is endless.

Behind the doors I know the crowds are there: seated, waiting and hoping. Nervous anticipation fills the room.

I am afraid. How will they react once they know?

Then I hear it. My thoughts are interrupted by a loud, ear-piercing roar. Shouts, cheers, claps — sheer joy. The sound of my heartbeat is almost outweighing the noise of the crowd. Then come the words I have waited so long to hear:

'Ladies and Gentlemen. I give you The Apprentice 2006. Please welcome … Michelle Dewberry.'

So now I understand.

This is how it feels to win.

Prologue

Walking out onto that stage was scary. Someone asked me how I was feeling and I remember saying, 'I'm sh★★★ing myself.' It was more acutely nerve-racking than the competition itself had ever been. Suddenly, millions of people thought they knew Michelle Dewberry. I was the quiet one: the Ice Maiden; the Silent Assassin; the Cold Fish; the Steel Pixie. So much had been written and said about me; so many labels attached to me. I was still the same person I'd always been, with the same strengths and weaknesses, but now I was also The Winner.

Ruth Badger, who'd been my friend and rival throughout the competition, hadn't talked to me much before we went on stage. That was making me feel even more uncomfortable. She'd wanted to win as much as I had, but in the end Sir Alan Sugar could only choose one of us; the other was going to have to make do with runner-up. I stared out at the cheering crowds. Then I caught sight of my family and friends who'd come to London to support me. My heart just lifted. I didn't want to be up there on the stage, I wanted to run over to them and hug them all and celebrate with the people who meant everything in the world to me – Mum, my brother Karl, my sister Clair and all my mates. My nanna wasn't strong enough to make the journey to London, but was watching at home. These were the people who'd been there for me throughout the hard times in my life.

I felt so elated. All I could think of was how I'd done my family proud. As for those people who'd said I'd never do it, that I wasn't very good – I'd shut them all up. Whatever anyone had chosen to write or say about me, Sir Alan had recognised my talent. There's nothing wrong with acknowledging your strengths, and I do believe I'm a talented businesswoman. It's great when someone else affirms that. For someone who is a successful, high-profile businessman to have acknowledged it in front of over six million people nationwide was just beyond words.

What *The Apprentice* taught me was the importance of believing in yourself. If you do, *anything is possible*. You can shoot and produce a calendar in three days. You can learn about cars and sell them in a real-life situation. You can put on a party, even if you know nothing about events organising – at a prestige venue like Tower Bridge, no less. You can do whatever you want in life – honestly! If you believe in yourself, you can do it all.

I'd never sold a thing to a member of the public – and certainly not to the trade – and yet I took on some of the country's top young salespeople and beat them on their home ground. I'm still immensely proud of that achievement. Around fifteen thousand people actually filled in the application form for series two of *The Apprentice*. Probably two or three times that number downloaded it from the website and thought about it, then decided they couldn't be bothered, or let it slip past the closing date. There was a gruelling series of interviews and assignments, which whittled us down to the final fourteen. And I had come first, out of them all.

Someone asked Sir Alan Sugar why he had chosen me. Was it because he'd felt sorry for me, as some of the critics had suggested?

'I'm a businessman,' he said. 'I don't pick people to work for me because I feel sorry for them. All Michelle's ever done in her life is work hard. She's become a great achiever. She's very focused, very determined, very organised. She's also ambitious. She's young and willing to learn. I think I've got the right girl.'

So how did I become all those things? People seem to assume that *The Apprentice* was the major turning point in my life. That's not so. The press sometimes choose to portray me as a Cinderella figure, plucked from the ashes by Fairy Godmother Alan Sugar, but that's really not how it was. I was the same Michelle when I went into that house as I was when I came out of it. At twenty-six, when filming started, I was the youngest contestant and had already been holding down a high-pressure job with a six-figure salary. *The Apprentice* was a great experience and, yes, it changed things by catapulting me right into the public eye, but it had little impact on who I really am and what I'm able to achieve.

The truth is my life had changed nine and a half years earlier, in October 1996. My sister Fiona died, in circumstances that have never been fully explained. The tragedy rocked our family. I was just seventeen when it happened and the memories surrounding that time are a blur of pain, confusion and misery. Her death left me with a sense of emptiness and loss that will be with me until I die. But ultimately it turned me into the Michelle Dewberry who won *The Apprentice*.

CHAPTER ONE

Fiona Kaye

I remember so clearly the last time I saw Fiona alive. It was my seventeenth birthday, 9 October 1996, and we were going out shopping in our home town of Hull to celebrate. I was looking forward to our day out. I loved being around my big sister. She was a wonderful person: kind, popular, funny, outgoing and caring. None of my family was tactile. There were no hugs and kisses at home – it wasn't allowed – but Fiona would fling her arms around me and tell me how much she loved me. She was my best friend – probably the best friend I'll ever have. I adored her. I still do, even though she's been dead for ten years.

Fiona had always been a bit of a tomboy. She wasn't a great one for dressing up or putting on make-up, whereas I was a bit of a Barbie, I guess, and she used to tease me.

'Chelle,' she used to say, 'life's for living, not sitting in front of a mirror all day. People should like you for yourself, and if they don't then you don't need them in your life.'

I'd always been much more of a girly girl. My hair was long and blonde, and looking back I can see I was very pretty in those days. I loved going out in skirts and heels and took ages getting ready. My dad wouldn't let me use cosmetics, but I'd usually sneak on a bit of make-up without him seeing. Fiona was different. If we were playing pretend games as children, I'd want to be the princess, but she'd be much happier in an action role. She had cropped dark hair and was usually in jeans or trousers. But that last day she was wearing a dress. And I was thrilled to see it was something I'd given her.

I was working in River Island at the time and we got free clothes to wear as our uniform, so I'd often wear them a couple of times in the shop and then pass them on to my sister. We were the same height and roughly the same size. I had this black dress which I didn't like, but Fiona really loved it. I'd never really seen her in a dress before. I can still picture it, clear as day. It was a cotton dress, with short sleeves, a loose collar, and black pattern details sewn into the material, right down to the ankles. When I gave it to her she was over the moon, making a big fuss about how pleased she was, trying it on and leaping around to show it off. She was like that, Fiona – what I call 'fussy' – very demonstrative, showing her excitement if something pleased her. It was part of her charm.

To my delight she was wearing it on my birthday, to go shopping in Prince's Quay. We jumped into a photo booth and got some pictures taken. As soon as the machine popped them out we grabbed them to see what they looked like. I was horrified. I thought we looked awful. I was peering over Fiona's shoulder looking all mean and moody and she looked like a real joker.

'That's *terrible*, Fee!' I shrieked. 'My God! I look like something out of a horror film. And it does nothing for you, either. It makes your nose look big and your teeth crooked.'

It really didn't do her justice, but then those instant photos never do. She was a pretty girl, was Fiona, always lively and bright and excited about what was going on around her. She didn't care what the picture did or didn't do for her looks. To her it was precious because it showed her and me together. She wanted everyone to see it. She had a mate called Donny who worked in Burger King. She dragged me in there, right up to the counter, and insisted on showing the photo to Donny.

'Look at this,' she was saying to him. 'Look, it's me with my little sister. I'm so proud.' I was mortified that she was showing it to her friends. But she was thrilled with it.

The next time I saw that picture, it was on the front page of the Hull *Daily Mail* alongside the report of her death.

Fiona was so happy that day. We did the usual things. A bit of shopping. A burger – poor old Donny had to have some compensation for being made to look at our mugshot! Maybe we had a drink somewhere. At the end of the afternoon we got on the bus to go home. I remember we sat upstairs towards the back. A friend called Natalie got on and joined us. Fiona's birthday was coming up so we were all yakking away about what we were going to do and where we were going to go. You know how it is. In no time we were at my stop and I dashed off, leaving them chatting.

I remember saying, 'I'll ring you, I'll see you later,' and them turning and waving to me out of the back window. Just an ordinary cheerful goodbye; her off with her mate and me running home to get ready to go out. No shiver of premonition that this was the last time I would see her alive.

A week and a half later, on 19 October, I was out doing my usual Saturday night stint of babysitting. There were two little kids I used to look after sometimes on the Gypsyville estate in West Hull. They were a family connection of my boyfriend.

One of the boys was playing up a bit that night. Once I got him settled I remember thinking, 'I'll just give Fiona a ring and find out what we're doing for her birthday and chat over the plans.' She was going to be twenty in three days' time.

I couldn't get through to her number. All I got was the engaged tone. I thought that was strange, because usually she had 'Call Waiting' and I knew she'd speak to me if she saw I was trying to ring her. The little boy was being a bit naughty and I was up and down getting him settled, but later I tried again and the same thing happened. I began to think that something wasn't right. We didn't have mobiles and I wondered if I should go round and see what was wrong, but by then the kids were in bed. I had no car and I could hardly wake them up and take them trekking on foot in the middle of the night across Gypsyville to Fiona's house. I kept ringing on and off throughout the evening. Deep down I knew something was wrong, but you know how it is. You put it out of your mind and get on with what's in front of you. Now, I'm always adamant that you should trust your instincts. That evening every bone in my body was saying something wasn't right, but I put it to one side. I don't suppose I could have done anything to change things, but the feeling of 'what if?' is terrible to carry with you.

In the end the kids' parents came back and the taxi arrived to take me home. It was quite late by then. Our house was pitch-black, so as soon as I got in the door I put the downstairs light on. The first thing I saw was my dad passed out drunk on the stairs. It wasn't an unusual sight. I knew from experience he was best left well alone. I remember thinking, 'What have you been up to now?' and just climbing over him to go up to bed. My younger sister Clair and I shared the front bedroom, so I crept in quietly to avoid disturbing her. We had a mirrored wardrobe facing the window. Anyway, as soon as I climbed into bed, the whole room lit up blue. For a moment I was disorientated, not knowing what it was, but then I realised it was coming through the window from the street and bouncing off the mirror. I got up and looked out and there was a police car outside our house. I wasn't unduly bothered but I thought it might be something to do with Dad being so drunk.

I went down to open the door and there was a policewoman on the step.

'I need to speak to your dad.'

'Well you can't,' I said, thinking of the comatose figure on the stairs.

'I have to.'

'You can't. I'll go and get my mum.' Mum's name is Glynis. In those days she went to bed early – she'd learned the hard way that it was a mistake to wait up for my dad if he came back from the pub in one of his drunken moods. I went up to Mum's bedroom and told her the police were at the door.

'Why?' she said.

'I don't know.'

'What have you done?'

'Nothing. *Nothing*,' I said, indignantly.

'Everyone's home,' she said, uncertainly. She used to hear the door banging and count us all in before she'd finally let herself drift off to sleep.

She came down and spoke to the police. I've blocked out what happened next. At some point they must have told us that Fiona had fallen from the window of her flat and was dead – but I can't remember their exact words. I just remember the pain I felt. We were all in shock. My poor mum went into her room, I went into mine and I sat on my bed, saying over and over again, 'That's my sister. That's my sister. It can't be right. That's my sister.'

Mum says that by the time I went to fetch her, Dad had crawled as far as the bathroom, taken his clothes off and passed out. The policewoman hadn't broken the news to us at once, but had insisted that it was important to wake Mr Dewberry up so they could talk to him. They tried, but they couldn't get any sense out of him. Mum had to bear the knowledge of a child's death alone, while her husband lay dead drunk and naked on the floor upstairs.

I didn't sleep at all that night. The next memory I have is of my dad's voice shouting – wailing, really – 'Glynis, Glynis.' He was sobbing like a baby. Suddenly I felt rage burning inside me.

People say they see red and that's exactly what happened to me. My stomach knotted and all I could think was: 'You *fucking bastard*. My sister's dead.'

I was angry with him for kicking her out, for rejecting her, for making her carry inside her all the hurt he'd doled out over the years. He was her dad, the one man she should have been able to turn to; the one who never let her down.

I'd never seen my mum have the strength to stand up to my dad through years of him hitting us. But that day she did. He was wailing and screaming, but she was hysterical with grief, yet over and above that she was angry with my father.

He was hysterical too. It was the only time I've ever seen him cry. Eventually he could stand it no longer. He ran out of the house over to the flats where Fiona had lived.

We still don't know for sure exactly what happened to Fiona. That's the hardest thing for me to bear. There was a police investigation, which meant that her body wasn't released for burial for several weeks while they went through the possibilities: accident, suicide or even murder. Somehow Fiona had fallen seventy feet from the window of her eighth-floor flat onto the road below. There were witnesses who claimed to have seen her climbing feet first over the sill and dropping down. One report said she appeared to hang there and then change her mind and attempt to pull herself back in. That scenario has haunted me ever since. I imagine her clambering out, perhaps to escape from someone who had come into the room. She's hanging there, frightened, hiding, waiting for him to go away. It's an October night, so it would have been chilly. I think of her gripping the sill while her little hands get colder and colder. Then, as she tries to go back, her fingers slip and she realises she's falling …

In the end, there was an inquest and an open verdict. They talked about the possibility of suicide, but the coroner said he was in too much doubt about her state of mind to be sure that she had intended to kill herself. I was the only member of my family to attend the inquest. My mother was sick with grief. And my father didn't want to know. Can you imagine how it feels to have lost someone so close to you and not to have the answers about how they died? It is soul destroying.

CHAPTER TWO

Being Good isn't Always Easy ...

My dad, whose name was Dave Dewberry, kicked Fiona out of the house around the time she was sixteen. I would have been thirteen. My dad often turned violent when he was drunk. And he was drunk often. Fiona, in those early days, was a rebel. To be honest she was what you'd call a troublesome teenager. She was the oldest of six children and often bore the brunt of Dad's brand of discipline. She stood up to him as much as she dared, but I know that she was as frightened of him as I was. By the time she got kicked out, she and my dad were rowing constantly. You didn't take that much notice of fights in our house. If someone else was on the receiving end of my dad's temper you just made yourself scarce and were thankful it wasn't you. We didn't tend to stand up for each other because we were too frightened.

The rows were about the usual kinds of teenage things, but Dad always took them to extremes. He was very anti-body piercing and she'd gone out and got her nose pierced. She used to take the nose stud out when she was in the house, but he'd seen her with it at the top of the street. He didn't want to touch it, so he wrapped his hand in newspaper and ripped it out. Another time she was standing on a street corner with her mates and my dad came past on the way back from the pub and caught her with a cigarette. None of my family ever smoked and he was furious. He dragged her home – by the hair, I think – in front of everyone.

Fiona used to wear his clothes without asking him. I think that's what brought things to a head between them. We were all supposed to be going away to Cleethorpes on an outing. Dad woke up, started to get dressed and decided he wanted his black cardigan. He was banging around looking for it, demanding 'Where's my cardi?', but of course it wasn't there. Fee had taken it and left it at her mate's house. It was a small thing, but I think it was the straw that broke the camel's back and he chucked her out.

In those days we were typical teenage sisters and I didn't really like her all that much. I thought she was a bit of an annoying big sister, I guess. She never thought I was cool enough to have around. She was one of the 'in' crowd and quite rough with it, while I was quieter, and I guess you'd say more geeky. She'd wind me up and call me names, so when she left my main thought was, 'Good-oh, I've got my own bedroom.'

She went first to live with my auntie Lottie, the estranged wife of my uncle Karl, Dad's brother. It didn't seem that significant at the time. I just remember Mum saying that Fiona wasn't going to come home. There were various episodes of toing and froing. Fee got work in some of the local factories –

Birds Eye was one of them – and Mum persuaded my dad to see her. She even worked for my father at one time. He'd started up his own business by then and was keen to employ family, but he and Fiona never saw eye to eye and it didn't last.

Things started to go badly wrong for Fiona between the ages of sixteen and eighteen. She met a woman who I'll just call 'Karen'. She befriended my sister and offered her a room in a house. At first the rent was reasonable, but bit by bit she'd explain to Fiona that she needed to increase it. In the end she was charging Fiona something like £65 a week. Fiona had nowhere else to go and she trusted Karen, so somehow she had to find a way of paying what she was asked. Karen probably lent her a bit of money to 'help her out' and Fiona ended up in her debt. There's no doubt in my mind that Fiona was desperate to feel someone cared for her – my father's speciality was making us feel unlovable. So she was especially vulnerable.

Eventually, Fiona became desperate to retain a roof over her head and someone suggested escort work, which was what she did. Fiona didn't like doing it, but it developed into something else. She hated the work, but she needed the money. She couldn't earn nearly as much working in a factory and she had no qualifications to help her look for something better. So to escape from what she was doing someone introduced her to drugs. In the circles Fiona was moving in by then, doing drugs was nothing unusual. She was trapped in a vicious circle. She was young – not even legally entitled to vote or buy drink – yet she was having to deal with the fall-out from a very hard, adult way of life. She couldn't come back: she was terrified of our dad. She'd stood up to him at home, but the emotional battering she'd received had left scars that lasted far longer than any bruises Dad had given her. She'd even dropped the name Dewberry and called herself 'Fiona Kaye', Kaye being her middle name.

Somehow, through all her own problems, Fee was able to become a great support to me. After she left home our friend-ship developed in secret – God only knows what my dad would have done if he'd found out I was sneaking off to meet her. She never let the bad things in her world touch me. When I was with her I felt so safe. I knew she'd kill anyone who tried to hurt me. She'd never let me get into any trouble. She was so protective of me. She wasn't deluded. She knew what she was doing was wrong and she wasn't proud of it. She loved me a lot and there are not many people I can genuinely say have loved me unconditionally.

Fiona may have found herself far deeper in that world than she'd intended, but she was a fighter. She realised that she was in trouble and went to Women's Aid for help. It took a lot of courage and strength of will, but she recognised the company she was keeping and the circles she was moving in were the path to destruction. She was eighteen when Women's Aid helped her find a place in a battered wives' refuge in Scarborough. We used to write to each other. I treasure the cards and letters I have from her, mostly written late at night on pieces of lined paper torn from exercise pads.

To begin with I found visiting her in the refuge was scary, because I'd spent some of my early years in domestic violence refuges and it brought unwelcome memories flooding back. I remember seeing one woman there who only had one eye, because her husband had gouged the other out with a screw-driver. Things like that frightened me, but Fiona used to put a brave face on it and pretend that everything was all right.

That room in Scarborough was in a huge old house. To get to it you had to walk over Valley Bridge, which they'd nick-named 'Suicide Bridge'; they'd put netting high up, curving over to try to stop people jumping off it. Then you had to go down lots of side streets before you got to the refuge. Fiona had an attic room right at the top. She had a bed and a sitting area with a couch in it. She was so proud of it. Looking back now, it wasn't very nice, but at the time I was really envious. I thought, 'Wow! This is well cool!'

I loved those times. I really felt I was bonding with my sis-ter. We used to go to the arcades, eat fish and chips, maybe go to a pub like proper friends do, and it felt really nice. Some of the happiest memories I've got have been in Scarborough with Fiona. One time she took me on some speedboats. Fiona was just in jeans and a jumper, but as usual I was all dressed up in high heels, a pink satin baby-doll dress and a white satin jack-et. The boat went really fast, the strap on my dress snapped and the wind pulled the dress down around my waist. I tried to pull it up, but I couldn't and I had to finish the ride in my bra!

Eventually she moved to a refuge in Hull and I used to visit her there. I loved just sitting in her room. Looking back, I guess the room was nothing special really, but to me, at the time, it was amazing. I used to love going round and just sitting with her. It seemed so grown-up. She had the newest hair mousse and face cream and perfume out on her shelves and I'd think 'Wow!' We weren't allowed to have cosmetics or make-up at home, so anything I'd bought for myself was tucked secretly at the back of a drawer. We'd go out together, too, to bars in Hull.

Fiona was really popular. She had friends wherever she went. If she'd lived, she would have had an amazing life and so many people would have been happier through knowing her. Through Fiona and the things that I saw and experienced, I learned not to judge anybody. Sometimes it's just too easy to pigeonhole people or write them off because of what they're doing or what they wear and so on. I just try to see the bigger picture. Any of my friends can come to me and tell me they're in trouble, getting beaten up, whatever – they could do anything and I wouldn't judge them. I hope that my friends recognise that if any of them were in trouble, my flat's an open house and a safe place for them. I'll protect them. That's the legacy Fiona left me.

The newspapers called my sister a drug addict and that really upset me. Defining her in that way gives the wrong picture of her; it goes back to what I was saying earlier about putting people in pigeonholes because of something they do. I see her as a person temporarily taking drugs because of the circumstances she was forced into. I know she was determined to regain control of her life, which takes real strength.

She was getting there. At the time she died she had her own flat, which she was renting from the council. She was very, very proud of it. I'd gone round and decorated the hall in smart Jeff Banks wallpaper and she loved it. Around this time, Fiona had decided she wanted to make a difference and help other people in similar situations to herself. She'd gone back to college and was studying sociology and psychology in order to become a counsellor. Her dream was to help victims of domestic violence and people who had generally fallen onto the wrong side of life. But tragically, on that horrible night, something had gone very badly awry.

⟨≈⟩

My dad had no idea that Fiona had been caught up in escort work. When he learned the full story from the police, his reaction was even more extreme. As I've said, on the morning after her death, he ran out of our house and over to her flat. But when he came back a few hours later, something had changed.

The tears had gone and in their place was a blazing temper. He'd gone to the flat and seen two policemen outside the building. There was a canvas screen around the area. He demanded to go inside, but the police told him he couldn't because there had been an incident. He was furious.

'I know there's been a fucking incident; it was my daughter that died.'

'You still can't go in, I'm afraid, sir. We're treating the death as suspicious, because of your daughter's lifestyle.'

'What lifestyle? What the fuck do you mean? That's my daughter's flat and I've a right to go in.'

I'm amazed that the police said anything about the case at that point, but they told him that she'd been working as an escort. From that moment on he decided that he had cried his last tear over her. None of us were going to be allowed to grieve because she, as he saw it, had let the family down in the worst possible way. He ran up into my bedroom and grabbed a picture I had of her from the chest of drawers. He couldn't understand why I had so many photos of her because he had no idea that we'd been close friends for the past four years. He snatched all my photos and I was trying to get them back out of his hands. He was screaming, 'She no longer exists.'

At that point I snapped and started swearing at him. How could he say things like that about his daughter when it was he that had kicked her out to earn a living the best way she could?

As the news of Fiona's death sunk in, I began to wonder if she'd been murdered. She was often frightened, perhaps because of the kinds of men she'd meet during her escort work. There were statements from people saying she'd been particularly worried around the time of her death. There was evidence that she'd been taking amphetamines, which could have made her paranoid – perhaps she imagined someone was after her. But that wasn't necessarily what drove her to the window ledge. I believe her fear had a strong foundation in reality. I won't go into my own house without locking the door behind me, and Fiona was the same. Yet on the night she died, the door to her flat was unlocked. She never would have been in that flat without locking the door – especially if she was frightened. She just wouldn't have done it.

The lady living below said that she'd heard Fiona arguing with a man. Someone else had seen a man running away from the flats. It was like one of those crime programmes you watch on the telly. You know, whodunnits – suspects, police appeals, scenes of crime and the rest of it. I felt as though I was trapped in a disgusting, sick horror movie. I kept thinking, 'Somebody is playing a joke and hopefully they're going to stop it soon.' It was terrible. It felt unreal. The longer the investigation went on, the longer it was before we could bury her. I went into a period of deep depression. I remember being at the police station almost every night, giving statements and asking, 'Have you asked this and have you spoken about that and have you found out what's going on yet? What about this and what about them?' I think I was probably a bit of a pain in the arse, with hindsight. It became a mission with me to find out what had happened.

CHAPTER THREE

I'll Be Missing You

Eventually they released her body for burial. I had to decide whether I wanted to see her. I thought long and hard about it, and in the end I decided I did. I went with some friends and it was the most heartbreaking thing I've done, ever. I had to have a drink before I could face going in. The pub was directly opposite the funeral parlour. I sat there thinking, 'Just one more drink, then I'll be able to do it.' I drank more and more, then eventually I thought, 'Right, this is it, I've got to go in.' It was late and pitch-black outside by then. I remember being surprised the parlour was still open.

We went in through the front door. It was just like a weird kind of house – an eerie, creepy, smelly, cold, horrible place. I'm sure it's not like that at all in the cold light of day. If you're detached from what's inside I expect you see it as perfectly clean and nice, but that was how it felt to me at the time. We sat there in the corridor, and I remember thinking the undertaker was really scary. I plucked up my courage and said I was ready to go to see my sister.

She was in what looked like a living room. It was dark, with thick blue curtains drawn over the windows and strange lighting. I took a few steps forward and peeped in the coffin. I was terrified. She didn't look like Fiona. I couldn't believe that I felt frightened of my own sister. I couldn't understand why I felt like that about someone I loved so much. Fiona had a little teddy – it was Sooty out of Sooty and Sweep – which she loved, and my mum had put it in the coffin and written a letter to go with it. It was heartbreaking.

I was crying and crying. I went out of the room, but after a while I went back in with one of my friends, a girl called Sam. I felt a little better then and less fearful because Sam was with me. Seeing Fiona's body made it all real. I had a sense of being so alone, like a small girl left to fend for herself in a world she didn't understand. My sister was the one that had always protected me, and she was dead. Who would look after me now?

I felt so vulnerable. For me, Fiona was like Superman. And, I thought, if she could die, then anyone could. That was when I started to view my life differently. I had thought this woman, who I adored, looked up to, respected, trusted, loved, would look after me. I had thought that no matter what, she loved me unconditionally and was never going to leave me. But she had. She was gone.

It was my job to ring round friends and break the news to them. I also got the job of clearing out her flat, because my mum was so upset. Losing a sister is bad enough, but losing a child is worse than anything. I remember walking in and seeing the Jeff Banks wallpaper I'd put up such a short time ago, covered in black fingerprint dust from the police investigation. There were marks everywhere where they'd used tape to lift prints off.

I had to go through her things and put her stuff away. It was so very sad. Eventually I climbed up onto the window ledge she'd fallen from. I sat and looked down and thought, 'This is what she saw when she was about to die.' It was so difficult to comprehend.

The funeral was at Chanterlands Crematorium in Hull, known locally as Chant's Crem. It was pouring down with rain, but it was incredible how many people turned out. The atmosphere was very emotional. Everybody who loved Fiona hated my dad, because he'd kicked her out. She knew some pretty tough people and there was a real danger of Dad being attacked. There were plain-clothes police at the house beforehand and they stood at the back of the crematorium to protect him. In the instructions for the funeral arrangements he'd asked in writing to leave the crematorium immediately after the ceremony – just in case.

I remember being in the cortège behind the coffin. It felt surreal. It was as if it wasn't me there at all – I was watching myself in the car, watching the coffin. I wore black leather trousers and a white lace shirt because I didn't want to look dowdy or depressed – because Fiona wouldn't have liked that. There were so many flowers laid out in the hallway as we were walking in. It made you realise how much she was going to be missed. More than forty memorial announcements appeared in the paper from friends and family. I've cut them out and kept them all. The crematorium was so packed that the doors were open and people stood outside the chapel, trying to get a glimpse of the ceremony.

My dad was paying for the funeral, so it was him who talked to the vicar. I could hear him saying things about this person that just wasn't my sister. They were talking about how she enjoyed swimming – but he hadn't seen her for years. I remember thinking, 'This is your daughter and you don't know anything about her. You don't even know what to say at her funeral. You never knew your own little girl – and now she's dead.' That really hurt me. He didn't know that I knew her well. He also didn't know that Fiona and my mum had a special relationship. Fiona adored Mum. Mum had supported her lots since she left the family home. Yet we all had to meet in secret, to avoid him finding out. None of us was allowed to cry, not even her own mother. Orders of Dave Dewberry, father of the deceased. No tears. I don't remember Dad showing any emotion at all throughout the proceedings.

I chose the songs. We had 'Let's Stay Together' by Al Green and 'Son of a Preacher Man' by Dusty Springfield. That one was one of her favourites. I remember being in her flat when I first heard it. I was in the bath and she was on the couch. She called through, 'Oh, Chelle, I've got this song for you to listen to. It's really *amazing*. Listen to the lyrics – you've got to hear it.'

She put the CD on. I wasn't impressed.

'Fiona, this is absolute *shite*. It's old-fashioned and it's dull and it sounds like something from the seventies. What are you thinking?'

She laughed. 'It's just because you don't appreciate it. The lyrics are really nice and it's a really special song.'

Being good isn't always easy,
No matter how hard I try …

I've got that song in my collection now, but I never play it. I can't bear to. It reminds me too painfully of the funeral.

There are three special songs in my life that remind me of Fiona. The third is 'I'll Be Missing You' by Puff Daddy. When I'm feeling indecisive or unsure in life and don't know which way to turn, that one always seems to play. I was once in an Italian restaurant, stressing about some crisis or other in my life, and they were playing this daft Italian weird banjo stuff and all of a sudden 'I'll Be Missing You' came on. I couldn't believe it. It was as if Fiona was across the table from me, saying, 'Don't worry.' Then the song finished and they were back to the banjos again, but I felt much better all of a sudden.

It happened again in the final of *The Apprentice*, on Tower Bridge, when I had a really black moment. I was exhausted and the task wasn't going as well as I wanted. We were on the bridge, waiting to go off and meet Gordon Brown, though we didn't know that at the time, and I was freezing. I asked the driver to let me sit in the people carrier while I waited for Ruth Badger, and because I was bored I asked him to put the radio on. It was really eerie. There was silence for a couple of moments, then 'I'll Be Missing You' started. It played all the way through and then it went off and some completely random unrelated programme was back on. It was as if it came from another time. I believe it was my sister's way of telling me, 'Stick with it. You've got to see it through.'

I miss Fiona every single day of my life. On what would have been her twenty-third birthday I bought her a card. I still have it. I chose it for the verse, which reads:

> *Hope you know how many times I miss you through the year,*
> *how many times I wish we weren't apart,*
> *How many times I reminisce about the days I've shared,*
> *the memories that keep us close in heart,*
> *How lovingly I think of you – especially today –*
> *while wishing you the best of everything,*
> *And hope you know I've always felt a sister like you*
> *is one of the greatest joys that life can bring.*

Fiona's memory is always with me, her name is tattooed on my body. I'll make sure that she's not forgotten – especially that Marc and Paul, who were very young when she died, don't forget their eldest sister who's in heaven.

Fiona and I shared so many childhood experiences. I fully understand what Fiona went through at home, because, as I grew up, it was similar for me. But now I realise that Fiona's death also eventually gave me the impetus to turn my life around.

CHAPTER FOUR

Daddy's Dream Girl

My life began on 9 October 1979 in Beverley Westwood Hospital. It wasn't an easy labour; they had to use suction forceps to help me out. Mum had been ill when she had Fiona, and because of that I had to be induced. Dad wasn't at the hospital. He was in his usual place on the terraces at Boothferry Park. Hull City are playing at home to Sheffield Wednesday. The Tigers, as Hull were nicknamed, were lying seventh in Division 3; Wednesday were two places above.

Dave Dewberry, my father, was notorious among Tigers fans in the seventies. He'd been part of a skinhead gang called the Monte Carlo Mob, who met at the Monte Carlo Café in Osbourne Street – a rough and run-down area of town. The Hull mobs became well known for violence on and off the terraces, and at one time the gang my dad was in had the hardest reputation of them all. 'The boys', as they were known, had nicknames. Dad's was 'Brains'. He always liked to be in the thick of things, standing in the roughest part of the ground, drinking in the seediest pubs. Later on he became known for writing new songs for the fans to chant at a game – he'd hand out hundreds of copies on the terraces. He had several tattoos, most of them proclaiming his allegiance to Hull City. Some had been professionally done, others he'd scratched out and inked himself. His devotion to the Tigers went a lot further than skin deep; he'd insisted on having the outside of his house painted black and amber. Everything was in team colours, right down to the dustbin.

The world would pretty much need to end for my dad to miss a home match. Seeing his baby come into the world hadn't even come close. Children and childbirth were women's work. He'd let Mum struggle in to the hospital alone. She'd had to carry her own bag and take two buses to get there, but that was the way it was. Dad didn't drive and he wouldn't have seen the point in forking out money for a taxi.

He did phone the hospital to find out if the baby had arrived. When they gave him the news, he got an announcement put out over the PA system at the game.

'Congratulations to Dave Dewberry. His wife's just given birth to a baby girl. Seven pounds thirteen ounces.'

That was my birth announcement. You can imagine the cheer going up from the lads on the terraces. Dave carried on watching his team hold Wednesday to an unspectacular one-all draw. Then he went down the pub for a bevvy with his mates to celebrate. He didn't come to visit Mum and me until a day or so later. I don't know if it would have been different if I'd been a boy. I don't expect so. He hated hospitals. It was a phobia that led to a lot of trouble later when my mum was ill.

My dad was obsessed with Hull City. He'd insisted that Fiona's middle name should be Kaye, after the club chairman of those days. Dad actually asked him to be her godfather. He didn't know the bloke personally, but, to his way of thinking, if the man was Hull chairman, he must be a fit godfather for a child. Not surprisingly, John Kaye had written back declining the honour. He did, however, send my dad a scroll, signed by the entire team, to mark the event.

Fiona was just coming up to her third birthday when I was born. I was literally the child of Dad's dreams. When he was courting my mother, they'd been planning ahead, as couples do, and talking about their ideal family. He told her that one day he wanted a daughter – a little girl with blonde hair and brown eyes – called Michelle. When Fiona came, she had dark hair, so they hadn't used the name on her, they'd saved it for me. So in 1979, here I was, complete with fair hair and eyes that started off blue but turned brown in a few weeks, just as he'd planned.

As a child I craved Dad's approval. I think most people do. I'd like a dad who's proud of me, boasts about my success to his mates, comes round and puts up shelves or fixes things in my flat for me. It's only natural to long for that. And Dad – he wanted children who were independent, streetwise, tough, hard-working, high earners, able to make their way in the world. So how did things go wrong?

I want to be fair to my dad. It would be easy to turn this part of my story into a list of all the bad things he did, but I want to show the positive side of my childhood and what I learned from it. On the other hand, there's no doubt that our family life was one which included domestic violence, with him as the perpetrator. It's impossible to ignore that side of him. I wish I could say I fully understand what was going on in his head, but he wasn't the kind of man who sat down and discussed things with you. There was never any justification offered. At home, his word was law. You wouldn't think of questioning anything he said – you wouldn't dare. My mum thinks that he was born into the wrong generation. He'd have been more at home as a strict Victorian paterfamilias. I've come to the conclusion that he had strong values; he believed you should work hard, stand up for yourself and owe nothing to anyone. While his life view may have its merits, the way he instilled it in us was wrong.

My dad was born in 1952 at his parents' home on the Boothferry council estate in West Hull. The Dewberrys weren't well off, nor were they a warm or affectionate family. His father, Don, liked things done in the traditional way and firmly believed a woman's place was in the home. There's no doubt Dad got his own old-fashioned views from his parents. Their home had a strict, old-fashioned atmosphere to it. Neither grandparent on my dad's side was particularly warm or affectionate towards us.

My mum, Glynis Donaldson, was born in Hull in 1954. Her mother Jessie – 'Nanna' to all of us – still lives in the same house. Nanna came from the Rhondda Valley in South Wales, but my granddad Walt Donaldson was from Hull. Nanna has always been a great source of inspiration to me. She is the kindest person and never has a bad word to say about anybody. She gets more Christmas and birthday cards than anyone I've ever met. When she goes to the post office, which is about a two-minute walk from her house, it takes her about half an hour because she'll stop and talk to everybody on the way. When I was growing up, we had a great time with Nanna; she would take me to the charity shop to buy books or to the Carnegie Library in Hull. We used to love to read together. At Nanna's house I'd always be stuck into Enid Blyton or Roald Dahl.

Nanna's a strong woman. I have this memory of her taking me to a park near her home. My friend and I were playing on the climbing frame and some bigger boys came along and started walking underneath and looking up our skirts. She put on a steely face and told them to 'sling their hooks', even though she was an elderly lady and they were boys who obviously thought a lot of themselves. She was sweet, but tough at the same time. She was always there for us when we needed somewhere to run to.

My mum first met my dad when she was seventeen. She was out with a friend for the night and they tried to get into a nightclub called Daly's, but the bouncer wouldn't let them in because they weren't eighteen. They ended up at another place, called Malcolm's, and met up with a couple of lads. One was a sailor – my mum's friend got off with him. Mum paired up with the other one. Dave Dewberry was nineteen, at the peak of his skinhead phase, with shaved head, Doc Marten boots, braces, the lot. He had brown eyes, brown hair – not a massive bloke, but strong and powerful, and, as I said, well able to take care of himself. When Mum eventually took him home, Nanna and Granddad had a fit! But he had charm – the gift of the gab – and they carried on going out. Mum sometimes says that if that bouncer in Daly's had only let her into the club that night, her life might have been a lot easier.

They married on 20 July 1974, just after my mum's twentieth birthday. It was a church wedding in Hessle, just outside Hull, and after the reception the bride and groom went to Scarborough for a few days in a B&B. During their courtship, Mum says, there was little indication of my dad's temper. He hit her once when they were engaged, but he was so contrite that she forgave him. Apparently he blamed it on frustration because he was unhappy at having to wait so long before they were married. He was a drinker, even in those days. Friday and Saturday nights he'd be down the pub with his mates, and at the football on Saturdays.

Once they were married, Mum began to feel trapped. Dad had inherited his parents' view that you didn't have people dropping in at your house and you didn't invite them unless there was a very good reason, so she became increasingly isolated. She didn't go out to work – he thought a wife's place was in the home, especially when the children came along. Dad was free to go out and meet his friends whenever he liked, of course. He would invite them round very occasionally – when there was something like a cup final to watch on telly – but if he did, Mum would make herself scarce until it was finished. I think that's why she ended up having six kids. She was happy when she had a baby, as she felt less alone. Fiona was born in 1976, and then I arrived three years after her. Next in age is my brother Karl, followed by my sister Clair. Marc and Paul, who I still call my 'babies', even though they're now grown lads of fifteen and sixteen, came along later.

CHAPTER FIVE

Growing Up in Pitt Street

At the time I was born we were living in Pitt Street, which, for anyone who knows Hull, is just off Albert Avenue. Pitt Street was a no-through-road of terraced houses, and ours was the end-of-terrace, noticeable by its black and amber exterior. It was quite 'seventies' inside, with a brick fire surround and very old-fashioned wallpaper. You had to go through the kitchen to get to the inside bathroom, and my mum used to have those fly screens in the doorway that were strips of coloured plastic. I always used to pretend I was a majorette or a dancer and twirl around in the ribbons. I liked that kind of pretend game. I was always dressing up and clopping around in high-heeled shoes five sizes too big for me.

Outside there was a concrete back yard. Before I was born, the yard was shared with the next-door house – no fence or anything. But my dad got into a row with the neighbours, which culminated in a fight. It was even in the papers because they ended up in court. Dad would go out and have a few drinks and then he'd come home and put his music on really loud on the record player. His passion was Roy Orbison. The neighbours objected to the disturbance. That would infuriate my dad, so he'd turn it up louder. On one occasion, he started up a fight with the neighbour in the back garden; my mum went out to try and calm things down. Unfortunately for her, as she opened the door she was accidentally at the wrong end of a fist and she got walloped. My dad ended up getting bound over to keep the peace. They must have put a fence up after that, because I don't remember it ever being an open garden.

I shared a bedroom with Fiona and our younger sister Clair. We couldn't agree on a colour scheme, so in the end we were each allowed to choose a colour for one wall. They were really bold colours – one was yellow, another was bright red and none of them went well together. We didn't have matching bedclothes or anything, so it was a real decorating disaster. I remember coming home from school one day and my dad taking us upstairs and saying, 'Come and have a look at this.' He'd got new green quilt covers and a little portable telly. That was really bizarre. I don't remember us ever being allowed to actually watch that telly. He wouldn't let us. So I don't quite know what the purpose of it was, although I do remember that the room looked quite nice.

Alcohol turned my father into a Jekyll and Hyde character. His life revolved around the pub and when he drank he became violent. He hit my mother regularly throughout my childhood. I remember him once going for her with a belt and the buckle cutting a gash in her head. It wouldn't stop bleeding and in the end she had to go and get it stitched. He'd kick or pinch or poke us. He was always pulling my hair. I was terrified of him – petrified. He had this look that came into his eyes. Even though I haven't seen him since I was eighteen, I can still remember that look. He would squint and clench his teeth and that meant that whoever was in his way was in serious trouble. We all learned to move quickly. When my younger sister Clair was little, she didn't speak for ages. As a baby, whenever my dad walked into the room she'd cry until he'd leave the room. When she did speak, it was me she used to call 'Dad'.

By contrast, Mum was such a gentle person. She was the grounded one, the stable one, the thoughtful one. She was often baking and cooking, and was always there when we came home from school. I used to love sitting with her and my brothers and sisters, having tea together. My favourite meals to this day are still the classic dishes she made for us as children – beef cobbler, toad-in-the-hole, chicken pie. Everybody who comes to dinner at my house now gets cooked beef cobbler – it's definitely my signature dish. When she was younger she was nice looking: slim and blonde, but the years of violence and worry soon became etched on her face. She worked so hard to make our lives as normal as possible. Having six children is enough to wear anyone out, without the rest that she had to put up with. Mum always went without for us children. If we were having chicken and veg and there wasn't enough chicken to go round, she'd have just vegetables. Every time she went without so we could have the best of what there was.

One of Dad's eccentricities was that we weren't allowed to have any food that he didn't class as 'British' on the table. Pasta, garlic bread, Chinese, Indian or other takeaways were all forbidden. We had to eat absolutely everything that we were given. If someone dared to say they weren't very hungry – perhaps they weren't feeling well – they'd be in for it. His way of punishing us was horrible. I remember him doing it to us countless times.

Thinking about what he did still upsets me. It was so degrading. He'd push his chair back with a scrape and then come round behind me. I wouldn't dare to move, but my heart would be beating fast, waiting for what was coming. Then he'd grab my hair and smash my face forward, hard, right into the plate of dinner. Then he'd walk back to his place and carry on eating. Slowly, I'd lift my head up, my face sticky with food. I wasn't allowed to wipe it off. I'd be forced to sit in front of my brothers and sisters, covered in mashed potato and gravy, and eat what was left on my plate. Then I'd have to scrape off what had stuck to my face – and eat that too. I'd desperately want to cry. But if I cried I'd get kicked under the table, so I'd sit there gulping and hiccupping, trying to keep the tears back. It was utterly humiliating. No one else dared say anything because they were too frightened. If you dared complain that your food was cold or inedible, even after he'd rubbed your face in it, he'd force you to reheat it in the oven and eat it when it was all dried up. All he'd say was, 'I've paid good money for that food. You're not going to waste it.'

Dad's mental abuse was much worse than the physical. His nickname for me was 'Fat'. He used to say, 'Pass me the newspaper, Fat,' or, 'Answer the door, Fat.' The memory has never left me. Later, after Fiona died, I developed the eating disorder

Bulimia Nervosa. I'm sure that his nickname for me and those horrible mealtime experiences must have been a contributing factor.

It was Fiona who first told the authorities about what was going on at home. We were at primary school at the time. I was taken out of PE class and called to the headmaster's office. I was scared, wondering what I'd done wrong. There was a strange lady in the office, along with the head teacher and Mrs Dale, the Lollipop Lady, who'd always been kind to me.

'We've been talking to your sister Fiona,' said the head. 'She's been telling us about something that happened to her at home. We need to talk to you about it.'

They explained that Fiona had complained that Dad had hit her over the head with a dinner plate. Had my father done anything like that to me?

I wondered what to say. When you're a child, you're used to answering the questions that your teachers ask you, but it wasn't something I liked to talk about.

'Yes,' I muttered eventually. 'He has. He gets the plate and then he puts it in a tea towel and then he bangs it on my head.'

'In a tea towel?' said the lady, looking puzzled. 'Why does he do that?'

I stared back at her. 'He puts the towel round it so the plate won't break when he hits me with it.'

'Does your dad hit you anywhere else?'

I nodded. I could feel myself going red. I tried to explain how he would nip and twist my skin. It was so embarrassing. But worse was to come. The lady, who I found out later was a social worker, didn't understand.

'It's important that I get this absolutely correct, Michelle. Can you show me what he does?'

I shook my head. I couldn't do it to the strange lady. I knew how much it hurt me. If I hurt her I thought I'd get into worse trouble.

'Just show me, Michelle. On my arm. Just here.'

In the end I had to. It felt like a bad thing to be doing.

The whole family were put on the social services 'at risk' register. We were sent to live in a refuge in Hull. By then there were four children – my brother Karl and little sister Clair as well as Fiona and me. I can remember standing, looking out of the window because I wanted to go and play with the others, but our registration process wasn't finished, so I had to wait indoors. It was strange, thinking that this was where we lived now, with these other kids who I didn't know.

When Dad found out we had gone, he was devastated. He tracked us down to where we were staying and would hang around outside. When my brother Karl went out to play football in the garden, Dad would give him notes to pass to Mum, saying he was a changed man and begging for forgiveness. All he wanted was for us to go home.

After six weeks in the refuge, my mother decided to offer him another chance. Social Services weren't happy about it, but they promised to make regular checks. For a short while, it was great, but soon my father lapsed into his old ways. The pattern was repeated throughout my childhood. My father would drink and become mentally and physically abusive. When she could stand it no more, Mum would leave, taking us with her to a refuge or to my nanna's house. Social Services would investigate; my dad would plead for forgiveness and swear that this time it would be different. Eventually my mother would relent and we would go home.

Mum did try to protect us. She'd try to stand in front of us to stop him, but it was no good if he was in a rage; he'd just go for her instead. You might be wondering why on earth she took us back to him time after time. What alternative did she have? She had no money, no real friends, no job, no experience or qualifications and a growing family to support. It's a common cycle in families where there's domestic abuse: she wanted the children to be brought up by both their parents. She wanted to believe him when he promised it would be OK this time. I understand what she was feeling: the hope that the future would be better than the present. It had to get better, or how would you stand it? I, too, desperately wanted to be loved and to have a normal family life.

My father's treatment of her drained away all her self-confidence. She became a victim. She dreamed of getting us out, but it always seemed too difficult. Mum had a 'going away' fund which she kept hidden from my father. She put a tiny amount of money away in it each week, to try to save up for when we could have a life of our own. She hardly ever had any money so there wasn't much to put away. It was a small lifeline for us. Years later, when Fiona got her own flat, Mum used the fund to buy her a TV. I remember feeling lost because our only lifeline had gone, but so humbled by my mum, because again she had put her family before herself.

CHAPTER SIX

Streetwise Urchins

Dad wanted us to have a hobby and was determined that his kids were going to grow up tough and streetwise. At the age of five I was enrolled in karate classes, because he wanted me to grow up knowing how to look after myself. I didn't like it – what I really wanted to do was dancing. He always said that we needed toughening up. If another kid hit one of us, he'd tell us to hit them back twice as hard. If we ever got bullied at school, his fatherly words of advice were, 'Hit 'em twice as hard and it'll never happen again.'

We used to go out playing in our street with the other kids who were always around – my dad would call us 'urchins'. There was a black girl across the street from us. One day the police came to the house and said they'd had allegations that I'd called this girl some kind of racist name, not knowing any better in those days. My dad went mad – not with me, but with the police.

'Have you got nothing better to do with your time than to

waste your resources coming round knocking on doors about something a little girl has said?' My dad has a passionate dislike of police, social workers, hospitals or anything else involving authority. I think part of it stems from the days when we were moved to domestic violence refuges and put on the Social Services register.

It wasn't all grim. Sometimes the whole family would play board games together. We'd play Snakes and Ladders or Monopoly. It was great. We'd get big bowls and fill them with peanuts and crisps and the whole family would get round the table. Dad made us do it all properly and follow the rules. I used to love those nights, but they were very few and far between.

And of course we all had birthday parties, but only when my dad was out of the house. Mum would organise it, but everything had to be finished by the time he came back. He'd have been drinking, and anyway he considered children's parties strictly women's business. We'd play 'musical chairs', 'pin the tail on the donkey', apple dunking and a game where you cut fishes out of newspaper and had to waft them over the finishing line. Mum would make us brilliant birthday cakes. When each of us was seven we'd have a magician – always the same one for all of us. He was a puppet master as well. He'd do the same gags and the same stuff every time, and a Punch and Judy Show with a red and white stripy tent. She would also do great things with us for Hallowe'en. We'd make a pumpkin lantern and would often have a Hallowe'en party where we would get dressed up in costumes such as witches and cats. It was the same with Bonfire night. We would have a bit of a party where we had fireworks and played games. Those occasions were very special.

Like all children, we used to love Christmas. I used to dream of the fairytale Christmases you'd see in films. We'd leave out carrots and trays of milk for the reindeer and we had plastic Santa sacks that we'd put out to go along with the whole Father Christmas game. We'd wake up on Christmas morning and find that Santa had filled our sacks, so we'd run downstairs in a state of great excitement. We had to wait until everyone was in the room, then we used to open our presents. There was a tree, green plastic, with red baubles on it and a fairy. We kids used to make stuff at school, and that would be hung up as well. We'd have Christmas dinner really early – about eleven o'clock. Roast turkey, all the trimmings, and proper Christmas pudding that Mum would make from scratch. Afterwards my dad would go to the pub. And that would be it. My dad didn't believe in having family over or anything. We'd see my nanna for tea on Boxing Day, but Dad used to say Christmas Day was *our* time. Family time.

I went to Paisley Primary School. I adored my teacher Mrs Gale – she was lovely. There were guinea pigs and a sand pit and a kiln for baking clay. I used to be teacher's special helper, staying in at break to help her get jobs done. It was good to do something for someone and feel appreciated. I knew by this time that I wasn't like the other kids. They used to have sleepovers and talk about things they'd seen on TV. We weren't allowed to watch television, except for *Blue Peter*, which Dad had decided was 'educational'. Sometimes, if he was out, we'd turn it on secretly, listening out all the time, terrified that he'd come home unexpectedly and find us. If he suspected what we'd been up to, he'd feel the plug to see if it was warm. If it was, we were in serious trouble.

We weren't well off, but we weren't particularly hard up either. But Dad had decided he was going to retire at fifty, so we were forced to live incredibly frugally in order that he could. We were only ever allowed one light on at a time, so we all used to crowd together into one room. In the winter, particularly, we'd all go to bed at eight, even my Mum. The heating was on for about ten minutes a day. Dad would say, 'If you're cold, put another jumper on.' We couldn't even read in bed because we weren't allowed the light on upstairs.

Later, when we moved to another house, which was very close to Boothferry Park, my dad made us turn off the lights and open our curtains when Hull City played at home, so we had the benefit of their electricity for free. He insisted that Mum had to mend all our shoes, like a cobbler. She had a metal shoe form and had to patch up any holes with rubber and glue and hammer and nails. He'd also make her turn his shirt collars when they started to get worn. We didn't have a fridge – not for years and years. Dad would say his mother had a pantry, so that was good enough for us. It was only when he realised that a fridge would keep his beers nice and cold that he decided to get one.

When we bought soap, Dad would cut the bar in half so it didn't all get used at once. When we had a bath we were only allowed to use an inch and a half of water, ever, even up to our teenage years. We had to use little children's pans to rinse our hair – Fiona's was orange and mine was blue – so as not to waste water. My dad used to slice the toothpaste tubes open and spread them out flat to make sure the last scrap was used. There's nothing wrong with practising economy, but as usual my dad did seem to take it to extremes. His upbringing has left me feeling very uncomfortable with waste. If I want to leave my bathroom light on when I'm at the other end of the house, I do. I get a kick out of it, in a way. But at the same time, I feel a bit guilty. When I was in *The Apprentice* house, Ruth Badger had some body lotion, which she used and then put the bottle in the bin. I said, 'What on earth are you doing?' She said she'd finished it. I said, 'My God. If you put the lid on and turn it upside down overnight, you'll see there's another two days' worth of lotion in there.' She thought I was mad. I took it out of the bin and stood it upside down to prove my point. I just couldn't help it.

In Dad's view, anyone who didn't live like us was 'weird'. I grew up thinking people were odd because they had a whole bar of soap out at one time! Not that we were allowed round to friends' houses very often. We certainly weren't allowed to visit anyone who had a pet dog. That was another of my dad's oddities – he hated dogs.

He brought us up to be terrified of animals. If we were walking down the street and a dog was coming, he'd grab us by the wrist and force us to cross the road to avoid it. I remember once being down an alleyway, cutting through from my house to my friend's house. A dog started barking at me. I was petrified. I was literally rooted to the spot. I didn't dare walk towards it, and I didn't dare walk away from it in case it chased me. I just stood and screamed and screamed. Of course all that did was make the dog bark more and more.

Eventually a bloke came out.

'What on earth's the matter?' he said.

'That dog's going to get me. It's going to get me!' I was yelling and crying in terror.

The man looked surprised. 'It's not. Don't be daft.'

But I was past reason. In the end he had to lead me away down the alley. If he hadn't I don't know how I'd have got home.

Even now, I'm terrified of dogs. My best friend has to hold my hand and walk me past hers, even if they're on a lead. I ring her on my mobile before I get to her house, so she can shut them in the garage and come out and meet me and escort me in. My heart races and I start to sweat and feel sick as I pass them. I know they can't get near me, but I can't help myself. It's another thing my father conditioned into me.

My first toy was a teddy in Hull City colours – Mum knitted it a black and amber scarf. My favourite 'toy' thing of all was a school register she'd got hold of from one of those cheap shops. I used to write down my brother's and sisters' names, line them up and call them out – I always had to be the teacher. I loved that kind of 'pretend' game.

I think I always knew that I was going to be in business even before I really knew what that meant. From the age of seven on, my idea of good fun was a game called 'Leaflets'. I used to beg my mum to bring home as many forms and leaflets as she could find. I liked the passport applications best, because there were so many boxes to complete. I would fill out these forms myself, or get my sisters and brothers to do it. Then I'd check them and look at how they were laid out. I'd find myself thinking that some of them would be much better if they were laid out differently. I could see better, more effective ways of doing things.

When I was still quite young I would roam the streets and look for work. It gave me something to do, and I enjoyed the rewards, as well as the opportunity to learn new things. I'd go to the petrol station on the corner and ask them for a job. They'd take one look at me and say no. But I'd say, 'Your forecourt outside needs sweeping – I'll do it if you give me a Flake.' Then I'd go to the newsagent's and ask them for work. And they'd say no. But I'd look around and say, 'My favourite sweets are Tutti Fruttis. You've got a big box of Walkers crisps out there but your shelf is empty. If you want, I'll take the crisps from the stockroom and fill the shelves if you give me some sweets.' After that, they'd usually say yes. So from a very early age I learned the value of transactions. I've always worked hard. I suppose what I really wanted was for my dad to look at me and say, 'She's not as thick as I thought she was.'

We weren't encouraged to hang around the house. We were expected to go out, toughen up and, in my dad's favourite phrase, learn to be streetwise. In his drive to make us independent, my dad would give all us kids a set amount of money at the start of the school holiday to 'get out and do things with' – to go on day trips. He was very keen for us to use public transport and would send us out to learn how to use trains and buses when we were quite little. I'd feel people staring at us in the queue, thinking we were too young to be out alone. None of our friends' parents would let them come with us. He made each of us a notebook – he didn't buy it, he made it – and we had to track all of our money, noting down money in and money out.

We were sent to join local play schemes. One of these was at a place called the Lonsdale Centre. We did art, craft and activities like break-dancing, and they took us on a few trips out. I enjoyed it a lot. Dad was prepared to pay for that because it was interaction, going out and meeting people, going to places, doing stuff. We always had to have a plan for the day – we weren't allowed to stay in or sleep late or anything. If we couldn't prove we had plans of our own then we had to go to the play scheme.

Another skill Mum and Dad thought we should learn was swimming, so I started training with the Hull Olympic Swimming Training Team when I was quite young. We swam at the Albert Avenue baths. It was just across the road, so we went ourselves after school and at weekends. Breaststroke was my speciality, although we had to do it all. It was very competitive. We had to do laps, block dives, timed swims, the lot. They also had fun nights where you could play with the floats and things. I liked it, and I made friends with the staff so that if I didn't feel like swimming I could help out in the cloakrooms instead. Sadly, I had to give up swimming training in the end, because I had to have a mastoid operation to remove a lump in my ear.

I think this is an example of how my dad's intentions for us were good. He didn't want bored kids. He wanted children with varied interests and ambitions; successful achievers. He even used to come and watch us sometimes. Once, he was so intent on watching me that my brother, Karl, who was still a toddler, got out of his pushchair and walked all the way home, crossing a main road by himself and finding his way back. Instead of being cross or embarrassed, Dad just said, 'That's my boy!' Karl had proved he could look after himself. He was 'streetwise' at the age of two.

CHAPTER SEVEN

Desperate to Be Loved

When I was around ten years old, we moved to another terraced house, still in West Hull, but a nicer part. Dad was doing quite well for himself. He'd begun as a valve salesman, but after a while he started his own business and was able to buy the new house outright. This was definitely a step up. In Pitt Street, the door opened straight onto the pavement, but this one had its own front and back garden. There were conifers at one side and flowerbeds in the garden. Behind the house there were allotments and a big field, known as Riley.

Despite the fact that I wasn't allowed a pet, I always wanted one, and when I saw my friends having such great fun with theirs, I felt I was missing out. So I found a plank of wood at the bottom of the garden and named it 'Keisha'. I used to tie a rope around its neck and take it for walks along the 'tenfoot' – the alleyway behind our houses where the children used to play – or in Riley field. It was a big bit of wood – about five feet long – and the neighbours soon got used to seeing little

Michelle walking round with her strange 'pet'. But when my dad found out he went ballistic and took it away. He couldn't bear to think of me making an exhibition of myself.

Next door lived an elderly couple who we used to call Mr and Mrs B. They'd never had any kids of their own and they were like extra grandparents to us. To them it must have been quite a big shock when our tribe moved in next door, but they were always really lovely to us. Our two gardens were separated by a small wall and I used to put my roller skates on and pull myself up and down it, hoping that Mr or Mrs B might be around to talk to me.

Mr B was a passionate gardener and had a big greenhouse at the back, full of flowers. I used to go and garden with him. One year we grew a giant sunflower, which used to stand at the front of the two houses. It was absolutely massive – much bigger than me! I would spend hours knitting with Mrs B. She'd say, 'Look at this wool I've got for you,' and I'd be really excited. It would be bits, scarves, or odds and ends. I was always on a project to knit my baby brother a blanket. I don't think I ever achieved it, but I was always there, trying hard. We spent hours in their house. There'd be tea and biscuits. Mr B was into scraperboard art, where you take off the black surface to make a design in silver underneath, and we used to do that with him. I enjoyed doing it, but I'm not really artistic. What I liked best was being with Mr and Mrs B. They loved all of us. Even after we moved to another house we'd all get a card from them on our birthdays.

Next door to us on the other side was Mrs Taylor, and next door but one lived Mrs Taylor's daughter, who had kids called

Donna and Christian. They became our friends. We used to make dens and potions in Donna's back garden. I was always round at her house. There was a narrow gap between their shed and the back gate and we used to cover this up and make a 'ghost train'. I soon saw the opportunity to turn it into a money-spinner and started to charge the other kids to come and have a ride. You'd go into the gap and we'd have things dangling down that would touch your face, and others sticking out the side that would hit you and scare you. Donna and I would take it in turns to be the ghosts and scare people. We'd keep ourselves amused for hours with it.

Donna went to dance classes and she'd spend hours with me, teaching me steps and making up new routines. I used to dress up in Donna's dance costumes and we'd put on shows for my mum and siblings. When I had to give up swimming, I nagged and nagged to be allowed to learn to dance instead. In the end my dad gave in. I was ecstatic. It turned out to be something I was really good at. Before long I was getting 'blue ribbons' in my exams – the highest marks possible. I've still got those certificates. The dance school used to put on displays, but Dad never came to watch me dance. I guess he just wasn't interested, which hurt me a lot.

Donna's family were devout Christians. Their life revolved around the church and she went to a club called 'Saturday Superkids', but Dad didn't want us to go because he wanted nothing to do with God or religion. He didn't believe in God. Mum would let us go sometimes, without Dad knowing, and I used to love it. I liked Donna and her mum was lovely too. When you're missing affection at home, I think you look for it elsewhere and I tended to latch on to people who were kind to me. You look for love wherever it's offered when you've been cut off from the normal sources in your childhood.

Donna was never allowed to wear make-up or hairspray. She used to have big, frizzy, curly hair, but her mum would never let her put anything on it. One day I gave her a makeover in the bedroom, using all this mousse and hairspray. We were really pleased with ourselves – she looked amazing. I'll always remember going downstairs to show her mum. She took one look and said, 'Get back upstairs, get it washed out and don't ever come down looking like that again.' I remember thinking 'Oops …' and getting sent home pretty sharply.

Sundays in our house were horrible. My dad used to line us up first thing in the morning and march us up the road to visit his parents. On Saturday I'd spend my time desperately plotting how to avoid the visit – and my father when he came back later from the pub. The only way you could do it was by thinking of something he'd approve of – something that showed initiative. I might lie and say I was going on an outing – somewhere like Flamingo Land, where I'd have to get a bus or a train by myself, showing I was tough and independent. Most times, I wouldn't actually go. I'd leave the house and hide at the end of our street, wait for him to go past, then run home. My mum would be cooking Sunday dinner, which had to be ready at 11.30 in order to leave plenty of time for my dad to go to the pub. Just before they all got back, I'd run out again, hang around the streets and come home after he'd left.

Sometimes, when Dad was at the pub, Fiona and I used to spend Sunday afternoons listening to the radio. We'd put a tape in and have our fingers hovering over the pause button for when the DJ spoke because we didn't want any talking, we wanted to make our own music tape. Then we'd spend hours playing the songs line by line and scribbling the words down on bits of paper until we had learnt them off by heart. We weren't allowed to get *Smash Hits* or any magazines that had the lyrics. We were only really permitted a radio with a tape because my dad used to go on the Sunday Soapbox phone-in on Radio Humberside, talking about his passion: Hull City. He used to want us to record the programme so he could hear himself played back afterwards.

I remember sometimes when he came back from the pub you'd hear him singing, swaying down the street. One time all I could hear was chanting, and there he was, leading a procession of local lads in a conga, chanting 'Oooh, Aaah, Cantona!' He was a bit of a hero to them on that particular occasion, but of course it just filled me with embarrassment. Some days he'd come in and fall asleep – and that was when we'd feel our luck was in. One day he fell asleep in the bath – passed out cold. None of us could use the toilet because we didn't dare wake him up. The whole family had to go next door and ask to use theirs. My mum was so embarrassed, she lied and said our toilet was broken. She couldn't face telling them that my dad was so drunk we weren't able to use our own bathroom.

Hardly anyone outside the family realised what was going on in our lives. In the street, my dad would sometimes hold our hands. To a passer-by he'd look like a loving guy with his children. What they didn't know was that he was squeezing our hand so hard it felt like he was breaking the bones, muttering,

'You fucking wait till we get home, you fucking wait.' It would be for some ordinary thing that kids do – nothing really bad. Like when I used to pull the leaves off bushes and chuck them in puddles, thinking they were boats for the fairies. Anything we did could upset him – anything at all.

One day I took my little baby brother Marc out in the pram, to get a lettuce from the local grocery shop. On the way home, I didn't see that someone had kicked a milk bottle into the middle of the street. I went into it with the pram and the pram tipped over. My little brother's nose was scratched and bleeding. I knew I couldn't go home with him like that or my dad would go mad. I stood in the street, crying, screaming and shaking, just terrified that my dad would batter me. In the end a neighbour stopped.

'What on earth's the matter, luv?' she asked in a kind voice. 'Are you hurt?'

I managed to sob out my story. 'The pram tipped over. I didn't mean to. The baby's hurt his nose. My dad's going to kill me.'

'Never mind, luv,' said the lady. 'It's only an accident. I'm sure your dad'll understand.'

I refused to be consoled. I was thinking, 'You don't know what goes on in our house.'

In the end she took me home, because I couldn't face going on my own. She explained it all to my dad.

'Your little girl's had this accident. She's frightened that you're going to tell her off – but I told her not to be so daft. You wouldn't do that, would you, when she hasn't done anything wrong?'

Dad was standing there, looking like a nice agreeable bloke, saying of course he wouldn't. But I knew him better than that. I was dreading the moment when she went and left me alone with him.

As she went down the street, there was a silence. Shaking, I took out the lettuce and put it on the kitchen table.

'What the fuck's that, Michelle?'

'It's … it's a lettuce. My mam sent me to get one from the shop.'

That angry look was coming into his eyes again.

'You idiot!' he yelled. 'That's not a lettuce – it's a fucking *cabbage*!'

In the end I got an even bigger hiding than I was expecting because I hadn't known the difference.

~

Dad was obsessed with hygiene and fresh air. Every morning I'd wake up to hear him shouting, 'Get yerselves up! Are you going to lie in bed all day? Out of bed and get some fresh air down yer skull ends.'

I'd hear him marching down the landing and knew what was coming next. The window was right above my bed, so he'd barge into the room and stand on top of me – not on the edge of the bed, but literally *on* my legs – to reach the catch and open it. He'd balance on me and I'd wait for the daylight and cold air to pour in. My mum had put Austrian blinds in our room and he hated them. He could never understand how they worked, so he'd just yank the cord, more often than not breaking the curtain, and then throw the window open to its full extent. Even in his office, the windows had to be fully opened every day. I never quite understood why.

Dad didn't drive – in fact, I'm pretty sure he'd failed his test a couple of times, then given up trying. He walked everywhere. If we ever had to go on a trip, he'd make us walk to the train station, no matter what time of the day or night it was, or what the weather was like. It was a forty-five-minute walk. We hated it. The only time he would ever get a taxi was if we were going on holiday and we had luggage. He'd get one taxi and he'd allow one child to ride in it with him. But none of us wanted to go in the taxi with him – we'd all suddenly decide we wanted to walk with my mum.

If one of us had the slightest thing wrong – even a blemish on the skin – he'd make us use separate knives and forks, marking them with tape so we wouldn't spread 'disease'. He'd make us feel dirty and disgusting. None of us was prone to acne, which was just as well – we simply weren't allowed to have spots. If we had a cold or anything, he'd make us get up and get over it. Later on, when my mum was in hospital having a brain operation, he refused to visit her, in case he caught some kind of disease. She didn't have anything infectious, but he banned us from going to see her in case we brought some disease home with us. But I was older by then and I'd learned how to defy him. I went anyway, and took the younger ones on secret visits when he was at work.

Mum never used to have make-up or new clothes. She had blonde shoulder-length hair and a perm that always looked as if it was growing out and needed doing again. She was tired-looking and always skinny. She used to have to wear the same thing for ages and ages. She'd go without new clothes to make sure that we had nice things to wear.

I shared a bedroom with Clair. Clair and I came home one day to find that mum had redecorated for us. She was so pleased with herself. She'd found some wallpaper reduced to about 30p a roll and you could understand why. It was pink patchwork, with pictures of ladies in flowery hats all over it.

We didn't know where to look.

'Mum … it's *awful*! What are you *doing*?'

'Well, it was cheap. A real bargain. Anyway, it's up now. You'll get to like it.'

We didn't. I put up posters which were more to my taste: Paul Young, Madonna and Ryan Giggs. When Fiona moved out I had her room downstairs.

When Mum was pregnant with Paul she used to wear a white padded jacket to go out in. None of the other mums at our school had even noticed she was expecting, so when she turned up pushing a new baby, they all asked, 'Whose is that?' She had a big grey Silver Cross pram. Marc would sit on a black toddler seat and my sister Clair would lie in the shopping basket underneath while Fiona and I ran by the sides, so I think we were quite a sight.

There are three distinct types of looks in my family: one that goes with dark colouring; one that is very fair; and a third that is a kind of mixture of the two. Karl, the eldest of my brothers, is dark and as a child looked very similar to Fiona. Fiona was such a tomboy. When we were very little, Mum would dress me in a blue dress with a red belt and Fee would have a red dress with a blue belt and we'd both have long hair – mine blonde, hers brunette. But as she got old enough to have her own say, she had her hair cut short. Fee always preferred to be running around like a boy instead of looking like a girl, so we were totally different. Paul, the second youngest, has turned out to be a bit of a mix and so has Marc. When Paul was born he was a real outdoor boy and was never happy in the house. If the rest of us were out and my mum was in the house, Paul would never settle inside. Mum would have to leave him in the big Silver Cross pram outside, and if you tried to bring him in he'd scream. To this day he loves being out of doors. He's a love-able little rogue, out with a football under his arm as soon as it's light and rolling home whenever he fancies it.

Clair is blonde and looks strikingly similar to me. I even struggle to see which of us is which when I'm looking through old family photographs. I think she's grown even more like me as we've got older. Although she's like me in looks, she's grown up to be much more like my mum in character. She's such a good, kind person. She's studying to be a nurse and takes eld-erly or disabled people out in their wheelchairs. It really upsets her if someone in the street gives them an odd look, or does-n't speak to them nicely. She tells me off for swearing too much. She'll say, 'Why do you use those words, Michelle? They aren't nice. You shouldn't do it.' She uses expressions like 'Crikey Mikey!' instead. She wasn't one to confront my father – she'd try and win his approval by doing jobs around the house, but then she was a lot younger than I was. I became more rebellious as I moved into my teens.

Of all his children, Fiona and I turned out to be most like

Dad in terms of character. That doesn't always make for an easy relationship. For us it meant major trouble. Fiona was the first to defy him, and, as I've already described, got chucked out of the house. For me it was a long, painful journey to the point where I was strong enough to stand up to him – and to take the rest of the family to safety, to a new life, away from the shadow of his violence.

CHAPTER EIGHT

'Never mind your education, get yourself a job!'

By the time I moved to secondary school I'd realised that some elements of my home life were far from normal. Because of this, I felt kind of distanced from the other kids. I wasn't helped by the fact that I had to stay on for an extra year at primary school. I'm still not sure exactly why my schooling worked out as it did. I think it was because my birthday is in October, but I wasn't old enough to move on to secondary with the others in my class. It meant I ended up doing Year Six again, in a class with the younger sisters of my friends. It was unsettling. Combined with the upbringing I was getting, it gave me a sense of being older than my years.

My mum says I was 'a bit of a home bird' as a child. I actually liked her to ground me for minor misdemeanours because it meant I could spend more time at the house. As I've said, my dad didn't like us hanging around at home. There was certainly no encouragement or support with our schoolwork. No one studied at home when he was around. He would shout, 'Fuck your homework, get out of my house.' If he saw us with our books out, he'd yell, 'Never mind about your fucking education – go out and get yourselves a job.' It's hardly surprising that I developed a casual attitude towards school as I progressed through my teens.

At Paisley Primary I'd been a good student: reasonably quiet, but no trouble. I used to get good reports. When I moved on to Sydney Smith, the local comprehensive, I was put into the top sets for everything. I was intelligent enough for that to be the case. To start with I kept my head down and behaved, but as I progressed through my teens, things started to change. I messed around more and took very little interest in anything academic. The teachers used to say to me at school, 'Michelle Dewberry, you will be nothing. If you don't do this bit of homework, or write this coursework about William the Conqueror, you're going to achieve nothing.' And I used to just think, 'Yeah, whatever.' By the time I got to my last year I was skiving off almost all of the time. When I wasn't skiving, I would be in the classroom messing around and disrupting my fellow pupils.

I suppose my dad's attitude to our schooling was a reflection of his dislike of most forms of institutional authority. On the other hand, he certainly didn't encourage us to doss around and aspire to nothing more than a life on the dole. He was constantly drumming into us that if you wanted anything in life you had to work hard to achieve it. Don't owe anything to anyone. Don't waste money. Don't have credit cards or debts. Don't live above your means.

Fiona, being the eldest, was the first to have to pay rent to live in the family home. When she was thirteen, Dad found her a paper round, delivering free newspapers and leaflets once a week. We're not just talking about delivering ten or twenty papers – the round consisted of delivering about 160 of the things. She had to contribute some of her earnings as 'board' for living in the family home. When she gave it up for another job, Dad decided it had to be kept 'in the family', and, unlucky me, I was the next in line so it was passed down to me. Every Wednesday I used to wake in the morning feeling sick because I hated doing it so much. While I was at school, my poor mother used to spend hours and hours inserting the right leaflets and folding the papers so the round was easier for me. It wasn't just that I disliked the round itself, it was the fact that here was another thing he was forcing me to do against my will. I probably wouldn't have minded so much if I'd gone out and found it for myself.

When I was fourteen he gave me a job in his office. I used to get the bus in the evening after school and go and pack valves in boxes. Any orders that had come in during the day I'd box up, ready to be sent out, and take to the post office. He much preferred me doing that than spending time on my homework, and to be honest, so did I.

My first proper salaried job was at Kwik Save, when I was fifteen. I was on the tills on a Saturday. The only uniform they had for me was a size sixteen and I used to look ridiculous in it because I was a size six. I didn't really care because I was there to earn the money, not to look glamorous. It was boring, but I was bloody good at it. I had the fastest checkout in the store. I prided myself on getting the customers through quicker than anyone else. You could gauge how you were doing by the size of the queues. If someone seemed to be going faster, I'd set myself the challenge of beating them. Even as a till girl I had the drive that all successful business people need. Quite simply, I wanted to give the best customer service. I wanted to do the job I was paid for as well as it could be done. So what if it was only checking out groceries? I didn't want to sit on my backside wasting the time; if I was going to be there, I was going to do it properly. I'd like to say the supervisors recognised what I was doing and rewarded it, but if I'm going to be honest, I confess I had to make do with my own satisfaction most of the time. Let's face it, sitting at a till for hours on end is boring. Doing it faster or better was my way of getting through the day. If things were slack I didn't sit around filing my nails. I'd do some extra tidying or merchandising rather than hang around waiting for a customer to come in.

A job like that may not be interesting in itself, but it can be the means to an end. If the only end is making money, then fine – I believe you should do it as well and efficiently as you possibly can and you may find yourself getting offered more hours, or being picked to progress to a more senior post. If it's something you're doing because you want to progress, then use it as a chance to demonstrate your qualities as an ideal employee. Challenge yourself and you will grow. If you hang around saying, 'This is boring, I don't want to be here,' then you'll find the job far more tedious than if you throw yourself into it and invent ways of getting more done. Being the fastest, or best, or most efficient – or even doing things as well as you personally are able to will strengthen your self-respect and self-belief.

Those qualities then enable you to have the confidence and experience to move on to what you really want to do.

The end I had in mind at that time was earning money, so I started stacking up the jobs. On Saturdays, I had three. I started off in Kwik Save, worked in the kitchen of the Fiveways pub in the evenings, then went on to babysit later. I did the pub job on Sundays, too. I was too young to be behind the bar, but I was the chef – plus I did table clearing and so on. Once again, it wasn't rocket science, but it was all right and I worked hard. Each Sunday, I had to prepare endless plates of sausages and chips for the local five-a-side football team who came in for their dinner; it always used to amaze me how they could polish off so many. I used to fancy some of those football guys, and I wasn't too impressed with the uniform I had to wear to serve them – a red and white striped tabard, complete with a hairnet and hat. Looking back, it was really not a cool look, and I was hot and flushed from the deep-fat fryer. No wonder I never managed to pull any of them!

❦

There was never any let-up in Dad's campaign to rear independent children. Even when we went on holiday we were still expected to get out and fend for ourselves. Usually, our parents took us to Butlins. They may have been called our 'family holidays', but for large chunks of the day we kids were kicked out by Dad to look after ourselves. He would gave us 50p and send us off on our own. On one occasion we had nothing but the swimming costumes we were wearing – no shoes, no towel, no money – and he said we had to get on and make a day of it. It would toughen us up. It was so humiliating, to be a young teenager wandering around in nothing but a cossie. OK, we could go to the outdoor pool, but it was too cold to hang around there for long. We had no choice but to go to the indoor pool, or freeze. My brother, sister and I had to walk into the inside complex just as we were, which was OK. But when we'd stretched out the swim as long as we could, we had to walk out again, dripping wet, with no shoes and no towel to dry on. I remember being mortified.

Once we went to Center Parcs and I remember Dad swimming with us in the pool and going down some rapids with us. We went for bike rides together. I really loved the time we spent there, and it was certainly a great step up from Butlins.

Dad didn't really have any concept of letting kids relax and enjoy themselves in their own way. As I've already hinted, I didn't always enjoy our family holidays. He'd always try to force us to do things we didn't want to. If we went to the entertainment hall in the evening and there was a dance floor, he'd say, 'Why are all the other fucking kids up there and you aren't? Why do you want to be sitting at a table with me? Get up and dance and enjoy yourselves.'

I remember Clair and me dragging ourselves up to shuffle around to Black Lace's 'Agadoo'. Every time I hear that song it brings back memories of this mortified child at Butlins; forced to get up on the dance floor, head down, trying not to be noticed. Normally I liked dancing, but it was the same old thing – I hated being forced to do it. It was the same with the karate tournaments he'd make us take part in. My heart wasn't in it. The instructor, who was Dad's friend, used to say, 'Your girls haven't got it in them, Dave, not really. They're too weak. They're only little girls. You're expecting too much too soon.' But of course he took no notice.

On holiday we played Swingball. That was one thing I really enjoyed. It was the best thing about Butlins. I'd take on the Swingball challenge and no one could beat me, not even my dad. I can still do it. When I go home, my brothers have still got a Swingball pole and I challenge all of them. I haven't lost a game yet! I don't know why I'm good at it, but I definitely seem to have a talent. I was well proud of all my certificates from Butlins saying I was Swingball champion.

We also got taken on days out to Pleasure Island in Cleethorpes, which is a kind of family theme park. At lunchtime we'd sit in a row on this pebble beach. Mum would go to the shop and get a pack of bread cakes and a pack of luncheon meat, and Dad would start passing them down what he called a factory production line. He'd put a slab of luncheon meat in a bread cake and say, 'Pass it down, pass it down.' You had to eat it. We all hated it and we used to try and bury the meat under the pebbles. One time he found us doing it and we didn't half get a good smack for being ungrateful.

There were some great rides at Pleasure Island, but I've never been a great one for rides as they make me queasy. It was the same with Hull Fair. It comes to town on my birthday every year. I like the side shows, but leave the other stuff to people with stronger stomachs. One time I won a huge stuffed Winnie the Pooh, but my dad wouldn't let me bring it in the house because he said it would be 'infested'.

Hull Fair was the really cool place for teenagers to hang out, too. Everyone who was anyone at Sydney Smith always went. I remember going there one night with my friends and there was a very cool boy I used to fancy who had got on the 'Limbo Dancer' ride. I saw an empty seat next to him, so I decided that I was going to get on and chat him up during the ride.

'Don't be daft,' said my mate. 'You don't even like rides.'

'So what,' I said. 'I like *him*. I'll be OK.'

I jumped on and said 'hello' and I could see him looking at me blankly and thinking, 'Do I know you?' I never got a chance to chat him up because as soon as the thing started moving, I could feel the colour draining from my face. Within seconds my stomach was churning. It was awful. I was breathing in and literally swallowing my own sick to stop throwing up over this boy. I was never what you'd call a cool kid, but that would have been the worst move ever!

My best friend in those days was called Sheila. I'd been friends with her sister Hayley, but when I got kept back at primary school, I ended up in Sheila's class instead. She was a nice girl, but my friendship with her emphasised the difference between us. I'd often be sent to Bridlington or Flamingo Land by myself or with my brothers or sisters as part of Dad's campaign to toughen us up. Because Sheila and our other friends weren't allowed to go off like that or do the things we were allowed to do because they were too young, my dad would brand them as weird. If we said we'd prefer to stay and play with our mates, he'd yell at us, saying, 'Just because your fucking friends' parents can't afford to send them out for the day doesn't mean you're going to hang around doing nothing.' It was embarrassing.

As teenagers, Sheila and I used to go out together a lot. I was allowed out till whatever time I liked, as long as I didn't stay away from home all night. Sheila, on the other hand, always had a curfew. The reasons for the difference between us were brought painfully home to me one night when I went to call for her. As usual, she was arguing with her mum about what time she had to be home.

'How come Michelle's allowed to stay out late and you make me come home early? It's not fair!'

Her mother had heard it too many times before and obviously decided it was time to put an end to the whingeing.

'I give you a time to come home because I care about your safety. I love you. Michelle's parents obviously don't love her or they wouldn't let her stay out to all hours.'

I froze. Hearing her words hurt me so much, because it articulated the greatest fear that overshadowed my childhood: my dad didn't love me. I don't think Sheila's mum meant her words to have an impact on me – I think she was just trying to justify her own rules to Sheila – but I was devastated. Sheila was loved; I felt anything but. Yes, my mum loved me, I knew that, but at that age I couldn't understand what my dad felt about me.

When people tell you bad things, often they're what you hold on to, rather than the good things. It's like a shield, a force field – the bad stuff gets in and deflects the good stuff. Someone could say to you that you're thick and someone else might tell you you've done something well – but which one do you remember? You just listen to the one who told you you're thick. I remembered Sheila's mum saying my parents didn't love me – and I believed it.

CHAPTER NINE

A Dad Who Fights Lampposts

The first time I really stood up to my dad is engraved on my memory. Clair and I were lying in our beds, in the room we shared, when we were woken by screaming from along the landing. It was my dad – and he was in one of his tempers. We could hear that poor Mum was getting the worst of it. As I've said, we were terrified of him and always lay low once he started, but that night was different.

'You fucking bitch!' he was yelling. 'I'm going to slit your fucking throat!'

We listened in horror. 'He's going to kill her,' I whispered.

We could hear the shouting going on and on. I knew I had to do something. My heart was racing and I was sweating with fear.

'I'm going to go and make him stop,' I said eventually.

Clair was horrified. 'No, Chelle, don't do it. You know what he's like. He'll kick off. Please. Just get back into bed.'

'I can't,' I said. My mouth was dry. 'I can't let him kill our mam.'

Eventually I plucked up my courage and went out onto the landing in the pitch-black. In their room the shouting was still going on. I took a deep breath.

'You leave my mother alone, you bastard! Just stop it. Leave her alone! You're a fucking bastard and I hate you!'

There was a silence. It was almost worse than the shouting. I ran back down the landing. I slammed my bedroom door and leant against it with all my strength to keep it shut. I was terrified. When I thought it was safe, I crept back to bed. I lay there, paralysed with terror, thinking about what was coming to me in the morning.

The next day he just gave me one of his looks.

'If you ever try to pull a fucking stunt like you did last night, you're fucking in for it,' he said. That was all. No blows, no apology, no explanation.

It was never spoken of again.

Dad's business was going well. He bought a new house in a better part of Hull – outright, cash down, no mortgage. It was a brand new development by Tarmac on a smart estate, and while it was being built we'd go round and play in the shell, exploring where our new rooms would be. It seemed like a mansion compared with our other houses. It had its own driveway and a garage, four bedrooms, three bathrooms and a big garden. There was a park opposite. The only flaw in the plan was the neighbours. When they heard how many kids were in the family who'd bought the plot near them, they went to the builders and said they weren't prepared to live close to us and asked them to turn us down. Of course the builders refused, but the woman said to my mum, 'You should be ashamed of yourself. You should be living on a council estate with all those kids that you've got.'

Not surprisingly, our two families didn't talk once we'd moved in.

It was this house that was so close to Boothferry Park that we could use the floodlights to read by. However, around this time my dad's great love affair with Hull City was nearing its end. When a grand passion goes into meltdown, the fall-out can be acrimonious and this was no exception. The club had fallen on hard times. There had been a 'coffin march' through the streets of Hull, which my dad had helped orchestrate. Eventually he took it upon himself to put together a rescue bid. He actually put in an offer to buy Hull City. It was a big story in the local papers: *LOCAL BUSINESSMAN IN BID TO BUY HIS CLUB.* You know the sort of thing.

Outwardly, I think my dad was seen by others as a good guy. At work they must have known something of his eccentricities – for example he used to get the office junior to cut around any stamp that hadn't been franked, and stick it on an outgoing envelope with a Pritt Stick. But he had plenty of friends. He was always at Boothferry Road, writing songs, leading support campaigns; he always knew what was happening. He wanted to be in the middle of anything that was going off. He had to be the ringleader. Not just partaking, but leading the action.

To this day I've never met anyone as passionate about

anything as he was about Hull City. It bordered on the obsessive. But the great love of my dad's life rejected him. The club turned his rescue package down. Heartbroken and furious, he turned against the club that had been part of his life for so long. He set up a group called 'Tigers 2000' that was highly critical of it, and he took to sounding off against the management during his calls to 'Sunday Soapbox'. He never went to a match at Boothferry Park again.

He still loved football, even though he now hated Hull City. He also had a bit of money by this time, so he had season tickets for several big clubs, like Manchester United and Tottenham. I remember going with him to see Man U v Spurs. It was overwhelming to go to Old Trafford and be in such a huge crowd. I was wearing a Man U shirt and I think, for once, he was proud to show me off. I had been going to Hull City games with my mates sometimes. I quite enjoyed football, but, to be honest, I suppose I cultivated a liking for it so that my dad would like me. I liked standing in the same rough part of the terraces that my dad liked, because it was where the action was. The seated areas seemed very tame in comparison. Where my dad went, it was always rough. He'd find the roughest part of the stand, the roughest pub, the roughest dives. He was never interested in the nice family places where most people choose to take their kids.

His local in Hull wasn't the sort of place I'd want to go in, put it that way. He was no snob, certainly. He used to say, 'Michelle, I can go drinking in the roughest pub in town. I might meet Jack, the man off the street who's just scraped together the price of a pint, and I could spend my evening talking to him. Or I could meet a millionaire who's just become a club chairman and talk to him. No matter what you do in life, treat everyone the same, it doesn't matter who they are.'

Sometimes, when he went to Manchester for the football, Mum and I would go along and do some shopping while he went to the match. One time we went to meet him in the pub after the game and he was asleep. When you're a teenager it's not very cool to be seen with your dad, so I thought being seen with my drunken *asleep* dad had to be the most embarrassing thing ever. Little did I know what was coming. Mum woke him up and got him into the street so that we could go and catch the train. He was staggering around, weaving his way along the pavement – and walked slap bang into a lamppost. All of a sudden he started shouting.

'Fuckin' come on then, what's your problem? C'mon!' and staggered around swinging his fists.

I stared in disbelief. He'd whacked his head on the lamppost and thought it was a person who'd swung a punch at him. Now he was trying to make it fight back. He was so drunk he couldn't understand why it wasn't responding.

I silently thanked my lucky stars that we were in Manchester and not in Hull where my mates might see us.

CHAPTER TEN

Teenage Binges

In my last year of secondary school, I spent most of my time skiving. I'd go in, sign the register and then leave for the day. If I did stay, I'd mess around and end up getting sent out anyway. One of my favourite tricks was to find out if a class had a supply teacher and go in there. I'd make up a name and say I was new, that it was my first day. It seemed funny at the time. One of the two GCSE passes I managed was in business studies. I got a grade C and that was without doing any of the coursework. I just always thought I didn't need school – I was beyond it already. I used to look at the teacher and think, 'What do you know about business? You've left school, you've gone to college, you've read up about what business is and now you're teaching me about it in a school. Where's your experience?' My view was that I didn't need her to tell me about it; I'd go out and find out what business was for myself. I do now believe that everyone needs a basic education, and I wish I had spent more time paying attention in class.

Sydney Smith was OK as schools go, but it could be quite rough. There were lots of fights outside – people would say, 'Right – you and me, on the common, after school,' and they'd be scrapping away as soon as lessons finished. I remember being bullied quite badly by one girl and to this day I don't really know what her problem was with me. I expect it was over some bloke, but I honestly can't remember. She was known as a bit of a scrapper. But even when she left she carried it on. She'd ring me up at home and make threats, saying she was going to kill me, that kind of thing. After I'd moved away from Hull and was in my twenties, she'd see me round town and still shout insults and throw drinks over me. At the marina one night, she flew at me, punching me and pulling my hair. It was like a scene out of a movie. The DJ stopped the music and switched on the lights just in time for the punters to see the bouncers wrestling us out of the bar, me covered in 'sweet cider and black' and her desperate to get back at me. I was really frightened and very embarrassed.

Not being allowed to stay in our home, I ended up hanging around with my mates on street corners. I'd definitely describe myself as a bit of a waster at that time. I had no ambitions and no idea what I wanted from my life. In an ideal world, if you'd given me a nice couch I could sit on watching television with a few friends in a warm house, I'd have been happy to stay in. You don't really want to doss around outside all the time getting into trouble – for a start it's bloody freezing, especially in Hull in winter. But my dad didn't want me under his feet and I wanted to be well away from him. I was a typical teenager and I started going through a phase where I thought

I knew everything, like you do at that age. No one could tell me what to do. Me and my mates would get into random people's cars and just go for a drive because we liked the music they were playing. I wasn't allowed to wear make-up, but I'd put it on at a mate's house, or sneak out of the house without my dad seeing me. I still liked to dress up – I always refused to wear jeans, only leggings and knee-high boots. I was a very pretty girl and enjoyed being girly. I thought jeans were too masculine.

I used to hang outside the off-licence for hours, waiting for someone to go in and get me my Special Red or White Lightning cider. Now I think of it, I guess I used to drink a lot. One night we were on some concoction of Mad Dog 20/20 and QC sherry, hanging out around the Ice Arena – the skating centre – which was the coolest place to be on a Saturday night. The last thing I remember is passing out in a puddle of water outside the arena, followed by a hazy impression of being laid out along the back seat of a car. I couldn't even stand up.

My mum was woken up by this strange bloke knocking on her door saying, 'I've got your daughter in the back of my car.' Luckily, he turned out to be a taxi driver. Mum dragged me out. Apparently I was shouting abuse at her, the driver and anyone else I could think of. I literally staggered up to bed and collapsed. Mum left a bucket beside me for me to be sick in. The next morning I lay in bed, waiting for my dad to go out, because I didn't want to get up and face him. I was thinking, 'Shit. He's going to kill me.' But he didn't. When he did see me, he obviously thought it was quite funny. I think he patted me on the head and said something like, 'That's my girl.'

Looking back, I suppose I was lucky nothing too bad happened to me. You hear stories about youngsters being taken advantage of when drunk. At the time I hadn't thought of the danger I was putting myself into when I got so drunk that I didn't know what was going on. Anyone could have done anything to me.

⁂

My first boyfriend, the love of my life for several years, was called Lee. I met him when I was still at school. He was part of the 'in' crowd and everyone fancied him, including all the trendy girls. None of them could understand why he chose to go out with me. I used to get bullied a bit because I wasn't in their gang and I'd dared to take one of their boys. Going out with Lee made me semi-trendy, but only by association. I thought he was wonderful. He already had a child by another girl, and that really upset me. However, when you're desperate to be loved you'll take any scrap of affection that's offered. Someone can be ordinarily civil to you and you'll count that as really nice, because your view of normal has become twisted by what you're getting at home.

Saying I 'went out' with Lee gives a bit of a wrong impression. We had the most bizarre relationship, and never actually went 'out'. We just stayed in, literally every night. He'd take me to his home – he lived with his parents on the Gipsyville estate – then announce, 'Right, I'm going out, but you can sit here. I'll come back and collect you when I'm ready.'

(Steve Double)

Clockwise from top left:
On the beach, aged ten months.
With Carl and Fiona, just before my third birthday at our house in Pitt Street.
My first trophy, which I got for karate at the age of six. I'm with Jim Dunn, who ran the club, and I almost needed his help to lift it.
Aged three at St Martin's Playschool – angelic face but not so angelic behaviour.

Clockwise from top left:
Celebrating my thirteenth birthday in style with a Fizzipops tracksuit and perm.
Two school photos taken during my teens at Sidney Smith School.
The last picture of me and Fiona together, taken in a photo booth in Prince's
Quay, Hull, on my seventeenth birthday.

Marc and Paul in 1997 – my own two little Red Devils.

With my proud family after graduating with my HNC in Business. *Left to right*: Marc, Clair, me, Mum, Paul and Nanna.

Top: My first girls' holiday abroad, to Benidorm, with Kelly, Anne-Marie and Sam.
Above: Enjoying a healthy diet.

Top: On holiday in Marmaris to celebrate my twenty-first birthday. The badge ensures I remember just how old I am. *Above:* one of my favourite pictures of myse

Top: With my housemates in Finchley. I wasn't as cool as I thought, looking at my get-up. Fortunately the table hides my pink fishnet tights.
Above: My best friend Vicky, in Clapham.

With my father at a family wedding.
(Hull News and Pictures)

Hard at work during my days spent
on the checkout at Kwik Save.
(Hull News and Pictures)

He'd go out and leave me talking to his mum. Then, when he felt like it, he'd turn up and say, 'OK, you can go home now.' And off I'd go.

You may be wondering why I put up with it. At the time, I thought it was great. I can't explain how much I loved being Lee's girlfriend. I got to sit in his house with his mum and dad every night and be part of a real family. Lee might not be there, but I didn't care. I was one hundred per cent in love with the idea of being wanted by someone. They liked me and I liked them and that was all I needed to keep me happy.

Lee wasn't the ideal boyfriend. Our relationship was turbulent and he was very possessive. But at that stage I had no self-esteem, so I didn't really expect much from him. I thought he was gorgeous. Every now and then he'd tell me he really loved me and that would be more than enough. He'd write cards to me and say lovely things. Lee was the first man who was ever affectionate towards me. How could I walk away from that, whatever else he did?

On one occasion I was babysitting Lee's sister when he stormed in and started accusing me of doing something or other that he didn't like. He was in such a temper that I ran and tried to lock myself in the bathroom. I shouted to his sister not to let him come in because I was worried he was going to hit me, but she didn't understand this sort of situation in the same way I did. Eventually, Lee dragged me out of the bathroom and began yelling at me. It was the kind of thing he did, but at that time I didn't have the sense to see that what was happening was wrong, or the will to stop him doing it.

Around that time, I went through a phase of applying for

jobs as an office junior. I got nowhere, probably because I had none of the right paper qualifications. I used to get really upset and think, 'I know I'd be really good at this – one day you'll regret it.' Probably all they wanted was someone to make the tea and tidy up, but no one was prepared to take me on, even for that. With hindsight, the suit I wore for job interviews was probably a right mess, because I couldn't afford anything better. The jacket didn't match the skirt, but it was the best I could do. Lee and his friends used to take the piss out of me for trying, saying things like, 'Who do you think you are in your suit jacket, going for job interviews?' He couldn't understand that I wanted to make something of my life.

Lee and I never used to go out anywhere together or do anything special; we'd just stay around Gipsyville, where his family lived. There was a place there where people used to hang out – it was basically a council house an old woman rented where people used to hang around drinking, smoking and dodging the police. There was a friendly atmosphere there, and I wasted a lot of time mixing with the wrong sort of people.

I fell in with a crowd that was into overnight raves called Destruction – I loved music known as 'Happy Hardcore'. We used to go all over the place – Sheffield, Skegness, Doncaster, quite far afield – and I used to come home at all hours. I wasn't allowed to stay out all night; that was the only rule. I was really trusting of people in those days and sometimes it got me into trouble. One day, when I was working in a clothes shop, I got chatting to a customer. She said she was going to a rave that night and wouldn't know anyone – did I want to go with her in her car? I said yes. As soon as we got to Sheffield, it became apparent that she *did* know someone there. She'd obviously planned to meet this bloke. She disappeared off with him and abandoned me. There I was, miles from home, with no money and no way of getting back. I burst into tears. I had to do something, so I went round to different groups of people and explained that I was stuck on my own. They all agreed to chip in a bit of money to help me get home. By the time I had collected enough for the cab it was daylight. As we drove down the motorway I was thinking yet again that my dad was going to kill me, because I'd broken his one rule: *Don't stay out all night.* Somehow I managed to explain it away with some excuse about what I'd been doing, and I got away with it. As long as I hadn't actually slept away, that was OK.

When I was seventeen, Dad decided he would pay for me to have driving lessons. Unfortunately, I didn't progress as fast as he would have liked. My driving instructor was a woman who was very chatty and friendly but also easily distracted. On one occasion she got me to pull up at the side of the road and, instead of telling me to reverse around the corner, started asking about my hair colour! Dad thought I should be ready to take my test. I knew I wasn't. Later that day, he questioned me and I eventually blurted out the truth about the instructor, who was one he'd found for me in the first place.

Dad was furious, but it was me that bore the brunt of his anger, not the instructor. He either punched or kicked me in the stomach – I can't remember if it was his fist or his foot that did it, but it was agony. I collapsed on the floor, winded and gasping for breath. As I fought to get the air into my lungs he thrust the phone into my hand and screamed at me to ring and cancel the lessons there and then. I couldn't even speak, but I wasn't allowed to wait until I'd recovered. When the woman answered, I tried to gasp out some excuse, but no words would come. His blow had winded me so badly I could only croak helplessly. In the end, she rang off, thinking it was some kind of crank caller. I had to phone her again later and try to explain that I wouldn't be coming to her for any more lessons.

In the end I passed my test at the second attempt. I failed the first time because I didn't see a child approaching a zebra crossing and because I mounted the kerb a couple of times. After I'd passed, my dad bought me a brand new car. At first, he wanted me to have a white one, because it was more easily seen on the roads, but I'd set my heart on a red Vauxhall Corsa and he let me have what I wanted. Looking back, I can see that it was a very kind gesture. It's one of the things that puzzles me, because I don't really understand the extremes of his personality. Not many kids of my age get a brand new car given to them when they've just passed their test. Why did he decide to do it? Perhaps he wanted the world to see that he'd made it as a businessman and could afford to buy something for his daughter. Maybe he was proud that I'd passed my test, especially when he hadn't. Probably he wanted to give me more independence, in line with his thinking that we should be able to get out and about and fend for ourselves. Part of the deal was that I was expected to run him around. He had to go off to all sorts of places by train, early in the morning. I'd go out late, clubbing and fall into bed for a couple of hours' sleep, then he'd come and wake me up at about six o'clock to give him a lift to the station. I'd keep the heater on in the car all the way so I wouldn't wake up too thoroughly, then I'd drive home and go back to sleep again.

Lee used to try to do things to my car, because he knew it would wind up my dad. He would nick the keys, or take the car and drive it away and hide it. It used to make me frantic with worry. One time, after we'd been arguing, Lee grabbed for me and I tried to run away down the street, but he got hold of me, and was swearing at me. Then he pushed me over a fence onto the ground and I was screaming for help. A guy in the street came over to see what was going on. Lee turned on him and started shouting that he was going to kill him, so he backed off but it gave me the chance to break free. I had a friend who lived on the same street as Lee and in the end I ran to her house. I banged on the door. She took one look at me and rang the police. The trouble was, at that time, you could call the police in a situation like that, but they couldn't take action unless the victim pressed charges. Despite being really scared of how Lee had behaved, I didn't press charges.

Now I think, 'How dare he do that to me?' But I recognise that people will only treat you the way you allow them to. In those days I had no sense of self-worth. My self-esteem was so low that I just put up with his behaviour and almost thought it was normal. My mum didn't know the full story – I'd never have told her the details, never. I hid them from her. She was happy that I'd found someone I loved, so she saw no reason to intervene.

At one point during our relationship, Lee had a spell in jail. Before I knew it, my Saturday afternoons began to revolve around going to Hull prison, and – strange as it may sound – I used to live for those afternoon visits. I'd pick up his family, drive to the prison and sit around in the waiting room. The room was big, grey and cold. The prison officers would select visitors at random to be called through for a security check, which would involve being called into a side room, stripped naked and checked for any drugs or suchlike which they might be trying to smuggle in. All the time I was waiting, I would be terrified. It was so out of my comfort zone and I felt like I was somewhere I didn't belong. Thankfully, I never got called through. When we eventually did get called, I was always petrified walking past the cells because the men used to leer and shout disgusting things at me. Because the prisoners didn't see many women, I felt like their bit of meat.

The authorities used to keep you hanging around for what seemed like hours, but in a way, I didn't care. I suppose it was because I knew someone was actually waiting for me and looking forward to me coming. I felt important to Lee in that situation, like I was really wanted and needed. He'd write loads of letters, but of course they had to be hidden from my dad. If he'd known I was seeing someone who was inside, he'd have gone ballistic. Lee would send the letters to his mum's house and I'd collect them from there. When he came out he bought me a piece of gold jewellery – like a ring or a sovereign necklace.

When I finally told Lee that I wanted nothing more to do with him, he was distraught. He came over to our house, grabbed some knives out of my mum's kitchen and locked himself in the bathroom, saying that if I didn't want him nobody was going to have him. He told us he was going to slash his face in order to become so ugly that no woman would look at him again. Worried about how he was taking it, my mum called the police. As soon as he heard her doing that, he ran away. His mother sent a search party out to look for him. It was pandemonium. His sister came round furious that I'd upset her brother.

After *The Apprentice*, even though we hadn't seen or spoken to each other for years, Lee sold every detail about me and our relationship to the newspapers. The first time it was a big double-page spread in the *Sunday People* about 'My Sex Apprentice'. It was me. At the time I thought it was harmless. Then, as the weeks progressed, he started selling personal letters and cards that I'd written to him and it all got a bit more sinister. After I mentioned the less happy side of our relationship to the *News of the World*, funnily enough, he never sold a story about me again.

It took me several years to find the strength to finish with Lee. Our relationship dwindled into an on-off sort of thing, but even though we both went out with other people, he was always there in the background. That was the first of several relationships with men which have followed a similar pattern. I now recognise that I used to allow myself to put up with degrading behaviour because part of me secretly feared that I didn't deserve to be treated well.

Nevertheless, the nineteen-year-old Michelle who finally sacked Lee off was a different person from the needy schoolgirl who went out with him in the beginning. My relationship with him was one of the many things that Fiona's death changed. Losing her forced me to see many things with clearer eyes. It was, as I've already said, the turning point of my life. It gave me the will and strength to stand up to my father. But a transformation like that doesn't happen overnight. I definitely believe that, often, you have to hit rock bottom before you can begin the long climb up to the light.

CHAPTER ELEVEN

Rock Bottom

The first few weeks after Fiona's funeral passed in a blur. I was drinking heavily — whole bottles of vodka, martini or gin — anything to blot out the pain. I have no clear recollection of how life carried on for anyone else in our house at that time. I don't know if that's because my grief has made me blank the memories out, or because I spent so much time drunk, or a combination of both. They were dark days. I was so unhappy. I'd wake up in the mornings and feel that I had a sheet of steel weighing down on me. Everything was bad, it didn't matter which way I looked at it. Fiona was gone. I was empty inside.

I turned my anger inwards. I hated everything about myself. I hated my life, hated my job, hated my figure, hated the way I looked. I was seriously depressed. I could barely make the effort to get dressed in the morning. I stopped caring what I wore or whether my hair was clean. Basically I didn't give a shit what people thought of me because I didn't give a shit about myself. None of it mattered to me. I was ploughed under by the loss of my sister.

Work was a nightmare. At the time I had a job as an assistant in a clothes shop on Hessle Road, called NS2. I couldn't face going in and I ended up taking a lot of time off work. When I did manage to drag myself down there, I found that all I could do was just sit in the staff room and stare into space. I had no energy for anything else. I wouldn't eat. I wouldn't talk. I just used to sit there. I have to say that the boss was really understanding and supportive, and so were the other staff. I suppose they understood that I wasn't ready to be back at work, but was trying to turn up because I needed the money.

I started to have suicidal thoughts. All I wanted was for my life to be over and for everything to end. On several occasions I attempted to take an overdose. Each time I wrote a note to my mum saying I was sorry, but I couldn't go on. I swallowed down a whole load of pills and went to bed, thinking that at least the pain would soon be over. But it never worked. I'd wake up feeling sick and groggy and gradually realise that I was still alive and in my own bed. I'd think, 'Bloody hell, I can't even commit suicide properly.' These days, I don't take painkillers unless I absolutely have to and I never take paracetamol because the taste brings back the horrible, sick feeling of those pills in my stomach. I remember on one occasion I left a note on the bedcover, along with the CD I wanted played at my funeral. It was 'Bohemian Rhapsody' as sung by Braids: 'Mamma, life had just begun/But now I've gone and thrown it all away ... '

The words seemed to sum up how I felt about myself. It

was a cry for help, but I really do think at that time that I genuinely wanted to die. Those suicide attempts went deeper than a simple desire to have my pain acknowledged by others. I believed – I still believe – that I'll be reunited with Fiona after death and I was missing her so much. I was hurting so badly that I couldn't see the pain I would be causing the rest of my family. I tried to remember how devastated I was by the possibility that Fiona might have committed suicide. It's a terrible thing to have to live with. My mum and the rest of my family would have that to deal with all over again, if I decided to take my own life. I told myself that, ultimately, suicide would have been a selfish act. I love my brothers and sister and my family; I wouldn't want to do that to them. In the months after Fiona's death my own despair nearly overwhelmed me, but, in the end my feelings for them proved stronger than the urge to kill myself.

As well as the emotional distress, I was also suffering from terrible stomach pains. I'd been diagnosed with endometriosis during my teens and now it flared up badly. In a nutshell, endometriosis is a horrible condition when your body makes uterine tissue outside the womb. These cells respond to your hormonal changes in the same way that your womb lining does – but when it breaks down it has nowhere to go. The result is appalling pain. The more depressed I became and the more I drank, the worse my endometriosis seemed to get. Some days I was bent double in absolute agony. I can't find words to describe how bad it was.

The year before I had been into hospital for a laparoscopy under anaesthetic, and when I came round they told me that

I'd technically died. My heart had stopped for a few seconds, but they'd brought me round. The consultant came onto the ward and told us that the recommended course of action would be a hysterectomy. My mum was there with me, of course and told them that no way was I going to have that done. I was only sixteen. They told me I'd be unlikely to have children, and I was tremendously upset by that. I've always wanted a family. Knowing that it wasn't likely to happen was a terrible burden to carry on top of the feelings of hopelessness I was already suffering.

In an effort to keep Fiona close to me, I started hanging around with a lot of her friends. I wasn't well, but I got myself together enough to go out with them because I found a bleak kind of comfort in being with them and doing some of the things she might have been doing. We used to talk about her constantly. A lot of her friends were quite rough and ready, but they had genuinely liked her and missed her a lot. She'd been a very popular girl. They used to take me drinking in Hessle Road, which wasn't a very salubrious part of town, and we'd sit in all these bars, full of old men who looked as though they were permanent fixtures. Ironically, they were the kinds of pubs my father liked to spend his time in. I can see it was a real waste of life, but it was part of the whole bleak period, spending the day sitting drinking in rough pubs, feeling more and more depressed and thinking about Fiona's death.

I was shocked and really upset by the news that one of Fiona's close friends, called Rachel, had died not long after her death. She was a lovely, tiny little girl with loads of curly hair – you'd think if you saw her that it was too much hair for such a small person – and she'd given up the drugs scene. She was clean. For some reason, she'd decided to take one dose at a party, and it killed her. I think she must have taken her regular fix, only her body could no longer tolerate the amount because she was no longer using regularly. I kept thinking, 'Has no one learned from what happened to Fiona?'

I had a good friend of my own called Kelly who did a lot to help me during that time. Kelly was a really nice girl, with thick, curly, dark hair and we'd gone out and had a good time together in the past. Now she was around when I needed her. I grew really close to her whole family. I even used to call her father 'Dad', jokingly. They were a great support. I remember walking into their kitchen once and noticing the Hull *Daily Mail* on the table. Kelly's mum ran to hide it from me, because the front page was all about Fiona. She wanted to spare me, but I'd already seen it. I used to love going to their home because it felt safe and normal and I felt they cared about me. I'd sit in their lounge, on the sofa, unable to talk, unable to do anything. They would ask if I wanted anything – just a cup of tea, or something – but I couldn't even manage that.

It didn't help my depression when I broke up with the boyfriend I'd been seeing. I was devastated. He'd attended the funeral with me and now it seemed all the support and sympathy he'd offered was gone. I was so angry to think that the notice I'd put in the paper to mark her death had carried his name as well. I was at my most vulnerable and here, yet again, was a man treating me as if I didn't deserve anything better.

That year after Fiona died, I can see I went off the rails. As I said, I was drinking far too much. With the drink would come a loud, over-the-top confidence. If I was at a party or in a bar, I'd have to be the loudest person there, the most drunk person, the one wearing the most outrageous outfits. If a stranger saw me, they'd think that here was a pretty, extroverted party girl up for anything. It was just an act. Inside I was a mess. There was nothing behind the shell.

My attitude to drugs changed for good the moment Fiona died. From that point on, I despised them. But I was still hanging around doing things I shouldn't have been doing. I'm embarrassed to remember some of it. On one occasion I got myself arrested. I'd gone into town with a girl who wanted to do a bit of shoplifting, and she'd persuaded me to hold a pair of jeans up, pretending to look at them, but really to screen her from the security camera. I was arrested and taken to the police station and my mum had to come and get me. They let me go in the end. Mum was really annoyed, but I don't think I got into heaps of trouble because she knew I was a very messed-up girl. I certainly was not in a nice place, mentally, after Fiona died.

At some point, I started to develop Bulimia Nervosa, an eating disorder. I'm not sure exactly when it began – I can't even remember the first time I made myself throw up. No one really knew what I was doing. When you're bulimic you want to hide it from everyone. I don't know why exactly – perhaps it's the shame – but you do. I thought I was being very clever about it. I would calculate what I would do and exactly when I would do it. I used to make plans: 'If I have *this* particular food it's going to take this amount of time before it comes up. If I have *that* food, I can get it out earlier if I have a glass of water.'

It was really easy for me because Clair and I had an en suite bathroom, so I could just nip in and no one would know what I was doing. I'd be so quick the family would think I was just in there for a pee. I became an expert. If I couldn't get to the loo for any reason, I'd actually throw up in a carrier bag. I used to take one out with me, just in case. I thought I knew what I was doing – I considered myself a clever bulimic. I did some research and read that the stomach acid destroyed your tooth enamel, so I was always careful to rinse out my mouth and clean my teeth afterwards. I'd think that I'd be all right because the acid couldn't rot my teeth if I'd brushed them.

I was really skinny. I would eat anything and everything, but then throw it all up again. I would take laxatives – cram them down. The first time I took them, it was like a revelation – they had the desired effect! I used to think, 'Whoever invented these is a genius.' Then I discovered that they sold *chocolate* laxatives, which was just out of this world. I loved chocolate. And now I could have my chocolate fix by eating laxatives and then get rid of it as well. Amazing! Mum must have guessed that some-thing was going on. She would find the laxatives and take them out of my bedroom, but she never mentioned it to me. I think she was afraid of another argument, but she was doing her best to protect me. I'd go to the drawer, find they were gone, buy more and then hide them. It seemed perfectly logical at the time.

I couldn't see that there was anything wrong with what I was doing. Bulimia was my friend and I thought it was great. I'd been called fat – now I could make sure I had a slim fig-ure. My life had gone frighteningly wrong – here was an aspect of it that I could control. I'd been made to feel worthless – now I was cleansing and purging myself every day. I was far from recognising the condition as a symptom of any underlying problems. In fact I had a very long way to go before I saw that Bulimia was a problem at all.

CHAPTER TWELVE

Something to Aim For

I was sinking lower and lower, spending more time with Fiona's friends, more time drinking. I can't remember there being one particular moment when I thought, 'Right, that's it,' but I started to realise that if I wasn't careful, I'd follow the worst path that her life had taken – which was certainly not something Fiona would have wanted. I began to say to myself, 'Rather than sitting around feeling unhappy, thinking my sister died and I'm probably going to die too, why don't I do something to make her proud of me? Instead of accepting the view that my lack of paper qualifications means I'm too thick to get a proper job, why not turn it around? I know I can do better.' Gradually I decided that I would take control of my life, rather than letting it drift.

It dawned on me that I'd already technically died once on the operating table, but I'd been given a second chance. What was I doing wasting it? I had to break out of the downward spiral I was in. Fiona had died, but I was still alive and I realised that I wanted more out of my life than this meaningless round of drink and misery. I managed to get myself to the doctor. He put me on antidepressants, which helped. After a few weeks, I decided to come off them and sort my head out without medication. As I regained stability and energy I began to formulate a plan. I knew I was good at business – I've no idea how, because I'd never done it – and I was going to succeed. I decided I wanted to be a 'famous' business woman. I had a vision of me standing on a stage with people being really interested in and inspired by what I had to say. I wanted newspapers and magazines to write about my business ability and achievements. I forgot about that vision until many years later, when about six months after winning *The Apprentice* an old friend reminded me of how I used to tell all my friends that I would be an achiever, and the whole world would know about it.

I decided that I wanted to combine work with study. I knew that I needed to get some form of an education, for my own sanity more than anything else. I did a bit of research and found out about the Youth Training Schemes you could do. I'd already had one YTS job, in the menswear department of River Island, but I hadn't enjoyed it. I recognised it was business I wanted to be in and not retail. I found myself a place with St John Ambulance and enrolled for NVQs in Business Studies and Customer Service. St John Ambulance had just installed a new computer system and people were having trouble getting the hang of it. I took a look at it and made it my mission to make sure I understood this thing inside out and back to front. I read the manual from cover to cover. I switched the thing on and played with it. I kept exploring what would happen if I clicked this button or that one; how I could make it perform the functions it was designed for. Whenever I had a quiet time I'd be into this or that programme, getting to know just how it worked.

Once I'd mastered it, I wanted to show other people in the office what it could do. I put together a training course and showed the other staff how they could best use the system. They were really encouraging. Everyone kept saying that they could see I had something going for me and that I'd go far. It was great. It was the first time I'd felt really appreciated in the workplace or been given the opportunity to use the skills I knew I had bottled up inside me. It provided a distraction from my personal problems and a chance to prove myself. My positive input was at last reaping some positive rewards.

Once I'd started enjoying my job and excelling at it, I could see that work would be my way of making something out of my life. I formulated a career plan. I was determined to get the paper qualifications that I needed to give me the opportunity to use my abilities to the full, and my training gave me something to focus on. I achieved my NVQs and St John Ambulance gave me a permanent position as an admin assistant, earning £7,000 a year. I was overwhelmed. I owe those guys a lot. They kept saying that I had something special. They were the first employers to spot my potential. I remember asking them if they were sure that they wanted to pay me that much, because it seemed like an awful lot of money after my £35 a week on YTS! I'd been earning £65 a week at the clothes shop NS2, but I'd been prepared to take the thirty pounds a week pay drop in order to get the qualifications I wanted. That was my first lesson in having a long-term goal in mind. For two years I was paid practically nothing, but I knew I'd eventually be able to move on to jobs with a far higher salary.

After I won *The Apprentice*, I went back to see the people at St John Ambulance on my birthday, and asked them about their first impressions of me. The accountant, David, who'd always been really kind and encouraging while I was there, said, 'I did have a bit of a job persuading them to take you on, Michelle, because you were a bit rough round the edges. A bit of a rough diamond.'

I guess I must have been. I had no concept of business, so I imagined it was fine to go into an office and behave just as I did on the street. I didn't think of moderating my language. I had no idea that things were done differently at work, so it was a real culture shock for me. Luckily for me, they saw past the rough edges to the real Michelle underneath.

⁓

Gradually my life began to turn around. I never for one moment forgot about Fiona's death, but I came to recognise that, without a doubt, it was going to change the whole course of my life. I understood that she had been a good girl who had become involved with the wrong things and the wrong people, but who had struggled to turn her life around. The tragedy was that her life had ended before she had had a chance to do the things she wanted. It taught me that you can have the best will in the world, but sitting dreaming and wishing will get you nowhere. There is no point in having fantastic ideas unless you do something to implement them. I used to wake up and think to myself, 'Do you want to look back on your life and see that you've never done anything; never experienced what life has to offer?' I still feel that every minute of every day has to be filled, achieving something. To this day, I often can't sit in the house on my own in the evening – I get this feeling I'm wasting time. I have to go out and do something. Back then, the drive to make something of myself before it was too late started to dominate the hopeless despair. I experienced a mounting sense of urgency. I became fearful that I was going to die at any moment and waste this second chance I'd been given. I had to act now, before it was too late.

I developed a strong sense that life is fragile. We as human beings don't spend enough time being grateful for what we've got. We don't acknowledge who we are or realise how lucky we are to be healthy. And yet all these good things can be taken away from us in an instant. It's not something we can control. When the time's up, the time's up. I was driven by the fear that my life could end – and I'd have wasted it.

As this realisation began to awaken inside me, I started to regain control of my personal life. I started to enjoy myself with Kelly and other friends. I went abroad on holiday for the first time – to Benidorm – and had an amazing time. Other trips followed. I started taking care of my appearance again and going to the gym. Unfortunately, I began to take it to extremes. In addition to the Bulimia, I developed a severe gym addiction. I'd probably train three times a day. I'd be at the gym before work, squeeze in another session at lunchtime, go there without fail in the evening. I knew all the gym staff. It was extreme but it wasn't all bad. I was very fit and my body was in the best shape ever.

I was at my happiest when I was at the gym. I'd get on that machine and not stop. I'd pride myself on it. People would come, get on the machine next to me and get off again, and I'd still be going. Someone else would come, do their twenty minutes and go. Eventually the bloke would come to me and say they were going to close, and I'd still be running. And running. And running. It was such a buzz. I think I was addicted to being in control. My body was amazing. I might get tired, but it was all about keeping my mind busy. If I focused on the running, or the weights, I didn't have to think about the other things going on in my life. When I look back, it doesn't even feel like that was me. I wish I had half the energy that that girl had. Nowadays I pay an extortionate amount for gym membership and hardly ever go. I do sometimes think it would be nice to be just a little bit like that younger version of me with all her energy – but only a little bit.

I had also enrolled for some sessions with a counsellor. I realised I couldn't deal with all my emotions. I wanted to talk about my feelings and emotions and get help from someone. By the time my appointment had come through I had begun to fight my way back from rock bottom and I felt like a real fraud going to the sessions. My hair was clean, I had nice clothes on and I had what they perceived as a good job. I felt like I shouldn't be there. The one-to-one counselling was fine, but I wasn't sure about the group sessions. It was a bit like, 'My name's Michelle. I'm recovering from domestic violence, Bulimia and my sister's death.' But I think it all helped me gain the strength I needed to turn my life around.

Around that time I decided I wanted to be an air hostess. I was in two minds about it. I liked the idea of the job, but I was reluctant to do anything that would take me away. You'd have thought I was desperate to escape from home, but actually I felt very torn because I didn't want to leave my mum. Strangely enough, it was the first time I remember getting any real encouragement from my dad. He was actually interested in my job applications. It knocked me for six. I was looking for a position as a transport rep to start me off, as I wasn't yet old enough to go for air hostess training, but that was my ultimate aim. In the end, my desire to stay at home got the better of me and I went off the idea.

Once I got my full-time position at St John Ambulance I used my wages to fund myself through night school. I started by retaking my maths GCSE and I realised that the faster I could type, the quicker I could get my work done so I took a typing course too. It was a great decision because even to this day I can touch type, which saves a lot of time. Eventually, I decided I was ready to move on. I realised that there weren't any long-term career prospects in what I was doing, so I applied for another job – and got it. It was another admin job, still in Hull, but this time with the Advanced Barcoding company. It was my job to set up the technical help desk for anyone who called the company with barcoding problems. I was the only girl in the team. I had to understand the processes and set up a structured system of IT help, sort out the paperwork and make sure everyone knew how to use it. I was gaining confidence. In both this and the St John job I'd look at the management team and think, 'I could do that.' Sometimes I'd find myself looking at someone who I didn't think was up to it, and think, 'If you can do this job, then I can run the world, with my capabilities.' I just seemed to have an inborn instinct for organisation – a talent for knowing what needed doing and how a set-up could be improved.

Just after my eighteenth birthday, I found out that Kingston Communications were opening up a new division in Hull. When we were growing up I thought that Hull was the be-all and end-all, and that to be a success in Hull, one of the companies you should work for was Kingston. Whenever we were in class and the teacher asked what we wanted to be when we grew up, we would all say, 'We want to work at Kingston.' I decided to be proactive and wrote off to them asking if I could have a job. Not any job, though. I'd decided I wanted to be a manager in their new company. I wanted to take Hull's most desirable employer by storm! I knew I was really capable, I knew I could make a success of it. I thought I would do them a favour and let them take me on as a manager!

Well, not entirely surprisingly, they wrote back and said no – but they offered me an interview for an IT admin job, quite similar to what I'd been doing at Advanced Barcoding. It wasn't what I wanted, but I thought it was a foot in the door, so I did my homework and prepared an interview pack on smart marbled paper, pre-empting any questions they were likely to ask me. It had headings along the lines of 'Why I want to work for Kingston Communications', with summaries of the answers underneath. I made a presentation binder, handed out copies as I went into the interview and basically took charge. I answered their questions before they'd even asked them. I got such a buzz from it – it was really positive. When they called me up and said that I'd got the job I was over the moon. I don't know where I got my confidence from, because I was making a lot of it up as I went along, but I went into that interview full of self-belief – and it worked. My biggest tip for all stages of life is to have self-belief. If you're convinced of your own worth, it's easier to convince others. If you know what you're doing and where you're heading and you're confident in your abilities to achieve it, no one can do anything to distract you.

I took the job because it was a way into the company, but I knew I had the potential to be much more than an admin girl. Quite soon I was bored. I used to look at other people and think, 'You're really good, but I could be better. I know I'm better.' I was in the IT department, so I started asking questions, reading, studying what other people did and pestering my boss to let me learn IT. I asked if I could go on some training courses, but he wasn't really that keen as it wasn't part of the role set down in my job description. So I studied IT off my own bat. I befriended the IT manager, and he would teach me bits and bobs. I used to spend a lot of time with him after work. We would go through IT and computers and how they worked and he would teach me all about it and I'd back it up with my own research. I was there because I wanted to learn more and progress in the company.

Looking around and seeing what was what in the company,

I realised that a lot of the staff had only the haziest idea how the telecommunications industry worked. I decided to change that and used to hold training sessions in the boardroom to put them in touch with the broader picture of how telecoms worked and how their own jobs fitted in. It was voluntary, and as I was only eighteen, around ninety per cent of the attendees were older than me, but loads of people came and it was a great success. After loads of pestering, my director finally agreed to pay for me to take the IT exam I'd been wanting to sit, so I prepared myself for that, too. It was a Microsoft Certified Professional qualification in Internetworking TCP/IP on Microsoft Windows NT 4.0. It's a very technical exam, but it has some of the building blocks you need for understanding IT systems and networks. It's all about domain hosts and sub-net classes and Windows servers – it was a real challenge to me. People didn't think I'd be able to do it.

I had to go to Leeds for the exam. I remember leaving my house, nervous and excited, thinking: 'Michelle, when you come back you're going to be an MCP – no matter what.' I remember having a chat with the IT manager, my friend, and saying how full of confidence I was. I was studying all the time – I'd worked my arse off, to be honest – and I knew I was ready for it. I went up on the train, sat my exam – and I failed. I was devastated. The result had come through instantly and there it was – failure.

I knew that my boss wouldn't pay for me to do another course, but I refused to accept that I'd blown my one chance. I went to the lady on reception and asked if I could take it again.

'I'm afraid not,' she said. 'It doesn't work like that. You have to go through the applications procedure. There are forms to fill in and the process takes time. Also, your payment has to be credited through the company. They have to get clearance from the Netherlands – you'll just have to come back another time.'

'When's the next exam?' I asked.

'The next one? In ten minutes.'

'I'm going to sit that one.'

'You can't. I've explained, it's not possible …'

I was determined. 'Well,' I said, 'this is what we're going to do. You go and speak to your manager and tell him what I want to do. Don't worry about the money; I'm going to the cash-point. I'll pay you before I go in.'

I ran to the nearest cashpoint and back. The manager came down, but he said I wasn't going to be able to go back in. I insisted. In the end I managed to persuade him. I handed over the cash out of my own bank account. I didn't have time to be nervous. I went straight into the exam room – and this time I passed. The percentage difference between the two attempts was huge. For me the improvement in my mark demonstrates the power of determination. In the space of ten minutes I went from a fail to a great pass through sheer force of will. I went back to the Kingston offices floating on cloud nine. I remember going into the director's office and him shaking my hand. It was a brilliant feeling. I was a Microsoft Certified Professional, just as I said I'd be, and it felt great.

I have a determination to prove people wrong. If someone says to me, 'You can't do that,' then I will. If it takes me weeks, months, years, I'll work out a way of doing it. There are some who feel threatened by young, feisty people, and when they're threatened they try to pull you down. In a working environment, if someone does that to me, I'll just smile and be professional. But I'll go off and work out exactly what I have to do to prove that I can deliver.

It's all about turning negative experiences into positive impulses. Don't accept what people say without questioning it. Take time to consider what you're being told. Is it actually true? Does it really apply to you? Is someone putting a stumbling block in your way because it suits them, or because they haven't taken the trouble to think it through; or because that's the way things have always been done and they see no reason to change them? Evaluate the situation carefully. Is it what you really want? How will you achieve it? Make your own decisions based on your own sound reasoning. And then go for it. In the two years after Fiona's death I'd travelled a long way. But I was still at home, with the family; still living in fear of my father's drunken temper. The next step was to sort out our relationship.

CHAPTER THIRTEEN

Escape

My mind has blacked out a lot of what happened at home around that time, but I can remember how angry I was with my dad for throwing out Fiona and for his attitude towards Mum and the rest of us. As I got older, I'd answer him back more frequently. My mum would try to defuse the situation, getting between us and telling me to shut up and get myself off upstairs out of the way. But inevitably there were confrontations. During one row I must have brought up Fiona's name. I'll always remember the words he screamed at me in return.

'Don't keep on about that girl. It was the second happiest day of my life when I buried her. The happiest will be when I bury you.'

The tensions at home and the feelings surrounding Fiona's death also had an effect on my relationship with my little sister Clair. One day, I had an argument with her and lost my temper. I found myself screaming, 'If I had to lose a sister, why did it have to be Fiona, why was it not you? If one of you had to be taken, why did it have to be her?'

That broke her heart. Even remembering it breaks mine, and as I write this I feel so ashamed that I said it. I was hurting so much and looking for someone to lash out at, and on that particular day she'd nicked my lipstick or some other trivial thing and I lost control. I wish those words could be unsaid because I didn't mean them. I love Clair to bits. But neither of us will forget that moment. I can say I'm sorry over and over again, but the memory is still there.

I knew I loved Clair and I knew she wanted to be close to me. I really wanted that too – there is nothing more special to me than my relationship with my sister – but part of me was scared to give as much as she was giving me. What if I lost Clair? Not in the same way as I lost Fiona; but what if she died?

I began to think about how we could get away. My mum had no confidence in herself, no joy in her marriage and she lived in fear of my dad. Clair, Karl, Fiona and I had been dominated by his moods. My chief worry was the future of the two kids, Marc and Paul – my babies. Fiona was gone, Karl, Clair and I were scarred emotionally, but I became determined that those two boys were going to have the opportunity for a life of freedom and choice, without fear, that had been denied us. It was like a light going on in my head. I knew that if I could change things for them they'd have a chance in the future. If only I could get them away from my dad, they would be happy.

I talked to my mum about leaving him. She wanted to – she'd tried, many times – and yet she couldn't make the final break. She was worried about the future. She had no means of supporting the children. Besides, she was unwell. She had trigeminal neuralgia, a condition that causes extreme, shock-like face pain. My dad was always on at her because of how the pain made her speak. The intensity of pain can be physically and mentally incapacitating. The doctors decided that Mum needed surgery on her brain to relieve the condition. It was a serious operation and meant that she'd be in hospital for a good few weeks. She was working as a cleaner for my dad at the time, and he made her go into work the morning of the operation, to clean his office.

She was put in a high-dependency unit, in a room of her own. Seeing her so ill reinforced to me how much we need to be grateful for our health. Dad wouldn't go near her and banned us from visiting, because of his fear of hospitals. I used to go anyway and take the other children, in secret. We needed to see our mother and she needed to see us. When she was well enough to go on the ward, all the other patients were asking her, 'Where's your husband? Why does he never visit?' She was so humiliated that she used to say he was in the Navy and working away.

One Friday night, when Mum was still in hospital, I went out to a pub at the marina in Hull and met a guy called Dave. We exchanged phone numbers and agreed to meet up. On the Saturday I took the kids in to visit Mum, then went home and rang Dave and we agreed to go on a date later that evening. I can vividly remember the scene. I was lying in my bed. I had my bedside lamp on and I'd pulled the blinds down and poured myself a drink – Baileys on ice. I was really relaxed, and looking forward to my date, thinking it was going to be a fresh start, a new relationship that might at last work out.

I was disturbed by a crash from downstairs – an almighty bang. It was my dad falling through the front door, drunk. His voice thundered up at me.

'Where's my fuckin' tea? What have you made me? Where the fuck's my tea, you idiot? Where is it?'

All of the household tasks had fallen on me and my sister in my mum's absence. But I had nothing ready for him, because it was impossible to know what time he'd choose to roll home. I remember feeling terrified. I went downstairs. He stood, swaying in front of me, absolutely off his head.

'I want my tea. Where's my food?'

'What do you want?' I asked, hoping we'd have it in the house.

'I don't know. Fuckin' use your brains. Make me anything as long as it's fuckin' hot.'

I tried to think of something quick, so that I could get out and get away.

'Shall I make you cheese on toast?'

'Yeah. That'll do.'

I started making the meal. He stood watching. Then he began to have a go at me.

'I know where you've been today, you fucking bitch. You've been to see her. Haven't you? You've been to see your mother. You think the sun shines out of your mother, but you haven't made my tea ...'

He kept on with the insults towards my mum. The more he abused her, the more my stomach knotted. My mum was the most kind and gentle person, there was no way she was anything like he was calling her. I felt a surge of anger. I had the grill pan handle in my hand. His voice droned on and on, badmouthing my mum.

'She's diseased, that's why she's in hospital. You're taking my fucking kids to see that woman when I said you were all to stay away. Who do you think you are?'

Suddenly, something snapped inside me and I lost it. I swung the grill pan handle and went at him, screaming at him to shut up. But he was stronger than me and he pushed me back. My head hit the kitchen cupboard. The room started to spin. I was terrified. He was going for me and I was trying to fight back, but he was a big bloke in a drunken rage, and I was a slender girl of just nineteen – maybe not even a size six. He was hitting me, but hitting him back was like trying to stop a rhinoceros with your bare hands.

I broke free and ran back to the door to ring 999. The boys had been playing hockey in the street and their stick was propped up in the corner. When I picked the phone up my dad got the hockey stick and started swinging it at me. As I put my hands up to protect my face, he smacked the stick down and it hit my wrists, hard. My hands went limp like a rag doll's. They weren't broken – I think it was the shock of the blow. I ran into the street, terrified of what he'd do next, hyperventilating with panic. My face was covered in blood and my hair was coming out in chunks where he'd pulled it. I had nothing on my feet. I ran and ran until I found a telephone box, but I couldn't think who to ring or what to do. I put my hand in my pocket and found a piece of paper with a phone number on it. I stared at it. It was the number for Dave. Somehow I managed to dial the number. Hyperventilating, sobbing and gasping into the phone, I managed to tell him that I'd been beaten up and needed help urgently. The rest is a blank. Somehow I got to his house – I think he must have come to fetch me. It was hardly the evening out we'd both had in mind.

I called the police, and they sent someone round to see my dad. He denied everything, but when they saw what state I was in, they knew that something had been going on. I was in a real predicament. I had nothing with me – not even shoes or a coat – so they offered me a police escort back to the house to collect my things. I was terrified of facing my father, even with a policewoman and Dave to support me. Luckily, by the time we got to the house he'd fallen asleep on the sofa. I was so frightened of him waking up that I didn't dare put any lights on. Dave and I and the policewoman went up the stairs to my bedroom. I grabbed some bin liners and began stuffing whatever I could find into them – pictures of Fiona, clothes, any money I had, some shoes, underwear. I'd just come back from holiday and I had some bottles of duty-free booze, so I grabbed those too. Then we crept back downstairs. The policewoman was carrying the bin bag full of bottles for me and I could hear it clanking and chinking as we went. I knew by then that I wasn't going back – and this was my one chance. If I didn't get my stuff, there was every chance that my dad would just burn it or throw it away. It must have been such a funny sight, the policewoman clambering down the stairs with the Bacardi bottles clanging, all of us in the pitch-black, trying not to trip over each other.

We stopped off at a friend's house further down the street to discuss what was to be done next: there were the children to think of. My sister Clair was only thirteen. When she saw my car and the police car outside the neighbour's house as she walked home, she came in too. When she heard what had happened, she said she wasn't going back to my dad's house either – but we had nowhere for her to stay. We had to have a plan, rather than just taking her away from Dad. In the end we agreed that Clair would go home, just for the time being, and look after the boys. She would sort out the meals in the evening and get them up in the morning. I would take over once my dad had gone to work, come in and get the packed lunches ready and get them off to school. I'd also help to pick them up. We got a routine going, but without my dad ever knowing. He used to leave a note for Clair, saying she had to do the weekly shop and here was a list of what was wanted, but he'd only leave five pounds for her to get it with. He expected her to be able to manage a household and live really frugally.

The whole thing had to be kept from my mum while she was in hospital, as she would have been frantic with worry about it all and that would have had a bad effect on her health. It was important that she should recover and get strong again. I was hoping that I could persuade her to leave Dad and bring the kids with her, once she was well. In the meantime, I moved in with Dave, the guy I'd met the night before I left home. I would classify Dave as my guardian angel. If he hadn't taken me in, I don't know what would have happened. We weren't together long. When my mum got back on her feet, we broke up. Too much had happened too soon, and our relationship didn't have the chance to develop normally before we were thrown in at the deep end. No one will ever understand better than me how much I appreciate what he did for me. By taking me in he allowed me to formulate a plan and to get my family away from my dad. I was desperate and he was there to help. I know I owe him so much.

When my mum was strong enough to think about leaving hospital, I told her that I'd left my dad and that she had to do the same. She was terrified at the thought. She said that my dad would find her and haunt her. In the end I gave her an ultimatum: choose my dad or me. It sounds terrible, and it was horrible having to say it, but I did it because I believed I had to be cruel to be kind. I needed to force her into making a decision, for the sake of the kids. I had to be tough because I knew it was the only way. After much deliberation and, I imagine, soul-searching, my mum said she would leave. She decided she would discharge herself from hospital and come with me. Together, we planned the family's escape. We arranged that I would pick her up, we'd take them all to my nanna's and then sort it out from there. But on the day she changed her mind, as it was such a huge decision to take. Eventually, she realised it was the right thing to do, and we went ahead with the plan. I knew that my mum had to break this cycle of going back and making a 'fresh start', however hard it was. I also knew I would be there for her every step of the way.

So I collected Mum and brought her back to Nanna's, and then carried on as normal. I stayed at Dave's. Dad thought that Mum was still in hospital, and Clair and I carried on the routine of looking after the boys. I can't remember how long my mum was with my nanna but eventually, when she was a bit stronger, we decided the time was right to move on.

We waited until we knew my dad was at work and drove to the house. I helped her pack the most basic things for herself and the children, and we left a note. We then went back to Nanna's and collected the kids from school and took them back to Nanna's too. That experience felt so strange. I had so many emotions running through me. I was scared that Dad was going to come back, worried about how things would work out, and felt terrible thinking about how he would feel when he arrived back from work and saw the note saying that we were not coming home. I felt really sorry for him, but I knew that if the family was going to have any chance of a normal existence, we had to get away from him – the family set-up was just not right. Karl felt sorry for Dad too, and decided to stay. He worked for him and didn't want to jeopardise either his job or the relationship.

After we left and went to Nanna's, Dad tried to talk Mum into going back, but she held out, with my support. On Christmas Day, she allowed Marc and Paul to go to my dad for a visit. Karl had had Christmas dinner – a ready-meal – with him and then they went to the pub. Later that afternoon, Mum got a phone call from Marc to say he was frightened because Dad was drunk and had passed out on the couch. Mum told them to walk out quietly and come back to Nanna's. When my dad woke up and found they'd gone, he went ballistic, and rushed over to Nanna's house after them. He started hammering on the doors and windows, then pushed the door in, screaming at the kids to get their coats and shoes on as he was taking them back home. They were terrified. My nanna, who was eighty-two, tried to stop him shouting at my mum. He turned on Nanna, calling her disgusting names, saying she had brainwashed my mum. He kept trying to hit my mum on her scar from the operation, saying the operation had turned her 'doo-lally'. In the end the neighbours called the police, but by the time they arrived, he'd bolted.

We moved into a rented house. Karl decided that he'd had enough and asked if he could come to live with us too. My dad used to make Karl be the communicator. He'd force him to bring notes and roses round – he'd done that in the days when we'd stayed in the refuge. Karl just didn't like it. He was constantly caught between Dad and the rest of us. Dad was by this time trying to get hold of the younger boys as often as he could. I'd get a warning phone call from someone in his office, tipping me off: 'Your dad's kicked off – he's going to go and try and get the kids, he's going to try to snatch them from school.'

I'd have to go to my boss, in tears, and beg time off to collect my brothers. I'd call the school and tell them he was coming, but there was little they could do to stop him as nothing had been legally settled and they weren't entitled to deny him access to his own children. So I'd be involved in a desperate race to get across town and to the school before him. I remember being held up once, and when I got there they'd been taken out of class and were sitting forlornly in the corridor, waiting. Looking at them I felt so sorry for them and all they were having to go through.

If the boys were playing football or something after school, my mum would go to pick them up and sit down to wait on the grass outside. One day, my dad turned up and went over to speak to her. To an observer it would have looked like a nice husband and wife chat, but no one saw that he was standing on her foot, crushing it, so she couldn't get up. He stood there, saying, 'You're an idiot who can't survive without me. You've got to come back to me sooner or later. You might as well realise it now. Those kids are mine. I won't let you take them away from me.'

I don't understand why he was so determined. It seems bizarre. Here was this man, who before had often acted like he didn't even like his children, all of a sudden fighting for them.

Eventually the boys came out and Mum tried to get them home, cutting back through the school fields to get back to the rented house she was living in. But my dad went after her. He grabbed her, headbutted her in the face and split her nose. She struggled onto the street where the house was, when suddenly he caught hold of her and put his hands round her throat. God knows what was going through his head at the time.

Marc and Paul, who she'd just collected from school, watched in terror. Suddenly, Marc broke away and came running down to the house to fetch me. I grabbed his hand and ran up to see what was going on. Dad had pushed Mum up against some railings. She was crying and her nose was bleeding. I could hear him screaming obscenities at her.

No one was doing anything to help. People were crossing the road and walking past on the other side, like I might have done if there was a dog in the street. I ran at him and pounded at him with my fists, 'Just get your fucking hands off my mother.'

I was pulling at him, but he was stronger and heavier, and I couldn't get him off. I managed to yank her away from him and guide her up the road, with the boys following. He was screaming abuse after us. I got Mum into the house, and into the lounge, terrified that he was going to follow. Karl was in the kitchen. Dad came round to the back door and Karl stood in the doorway and said, 'Where do you think you're going?'

Dad said, 'I want to talk to Glynis.'

'Over my dead body. You're not coming into this house.'

Karl slammed the door in his face. It was the first time I had seen my brother stand up to my dad like that and I was so proud of him.

My mum was gasping and shaking. Her nose was bleeding. She had marks all over her.

'I'm going to ring the police,' I said eventually.

'No – don't. Please, Chelle no. He'll cause trouble. He really will.'

She refused to do it herself, because she was so scared, so in the end I did. He was arrested but released without charge. Once they let him go, he disappeared. Mum divorced him, and I've never seen him since.

Mum's a great inspiration to me. Nowadays she's this reinvented woman. She's really made something of herself. She's remarried and is very happy with her new partner. She's Glynis now, whereas before she was just Dave's wife and our mum. I feel proud that Mum found the strength inside herself to get out. To have six children, no job and no money and to leave your husband while you're in immense fear – I can't put into words how much strength that takes. Yet she did it. She has turned her life around. She had nothing, no qualifications, yet she's gone to college, retrained and works as an auxiliary nurse in the hospital. She now has lots of friends, hobbies and a great social life.

A little while ago, before *The Apprentice* was on television, my dad contacted my mum and asked if any of the children would be willing to talk to him. She asked us all and I was the only one who said yes. I would have liked the chance to ask him why he brought us up the way he did. There are so many questions unanswered in my mind.

Did he really think I was as useless as he said I was, or was it his misguided way of trying to motivate me to do better? Would he really be happier if I were dead?

All these years later I can see that many of his actions were motivated by his desire to instil into us a sound work ethic. He wanted us to be tough and independent, able to make our own way and earn a living for ourselves. But I don't understand why he did it by humiliating us and frightening us. I know I'm like him, in some ways. I know that part of the reason I am who I am is because of the lessons he taught me and the fears and insecurities he instilled in me. Somewhere inside him I believe he meant well.

His way of expressing his beliefs was extreme, but because of what I learned from him, I don't owe anything to anybody.

I strongly believe that if you want something and you can't afford it, then you should go and get a better job, or make do with something less expensive. I try to avoid getting into any debt, and I often wonder how people in thousands of pounds' worth of debt sleep at night. I know if it was me, I would feel very stressed. Everything I have is mine outright, with the exception of my home – and I've earned it through hard work and sheer determination. When I see how many people get into trouble with debt, I know that it's one thing my dad taught me that was right. There's a good chance he's heard about me winning *The Apprentice* or even seen me on it. There's no doubt that some of what he taught me helped me to win and made me stronger, but it was also that strength that enabled me to escape from him.

CHAPTER FOURTEEN

New Start

Soon after my nineteenth birthday, things were much more settled. I enrolled to take an HNC at night school, and for a while moved into the old family home, as Dad had disappeared. Mum and the younger kids were living in their own rented place and didn't want to go back, but I didn't want to leave the house standing empty in case it was broken into or vandalised – eventually it was made over to Mum in the end, through the divorce settlement.

Even in those days I did quite a bit to help people with career changes and job applications. I'd seen how it was possible to do it for myself, and I was pleased to help others turn their lives around. Friends would come to me and ask for assistance putting together a CV, or preparing for an interview. Together with the training seminars I was running at Kingston, it made me think that mentoring was something I'd like to be involved in. After all, I'd had to get on without anyone standing over me advising me. How much easier it would have been with a mentor on hand to discuss things with.

I wasn't doing so badly on my own. With my hard won Microsoft qualification I was given a position in the IT department, which meant I was writing databases and managed the network. But it wasn't enough for me. I was funding myself through a two-year HNC in business management in order to progress further. I realised that, as I didn't have a degree, I needed the theory to back up my practical experience. It was hard going, studying at night and in my spare time, but I loved learning about business. I realised that I needed to understand more about terms like profit and loss and the wider scale of things in order to get on. I have to say it was a little bit like my school-days. I was the joker of the class. I was always the one messing around, but I was always very clear about getting the work done.

The old fear of time running out was still haunting me. I got into the habit of making lists of what I'd achieved and how I was progressing towards my goals. I've kept a lot of these – in fact I'm still making them and updating them. It keeps me awake, wondering what I should be doing to implement the next plan. I always had career plans. My top tip is to write them down. Don't just have a vague idea in your mind about what you want to do – write it down, put it on a card and pin it up on your wall so you see it every day. Let it motivate you. I still use them. I cut out pictures of things I want – like a lakeside house – that I'm determined to get and pin them up in my office. Then, if I'm having a bad day or I feel like I can't be bothered, I can look at them and think, 'This is what I'm working for. I want to achieve these things.' You need to visualise your ideas; make them inspire you.

At Kingston, I pushed for promotion and was made a solutions analyst. I was sent on courses and attended exhibitions.
I'd look around at these places and find I was at least ten years
younger than any of the other solutions analysts there. At that
time the Internet service provider Tiscali were Kingston's
biggest client by far. They were a demanding customer and had
had a long string of project managers coming and going to
manage their account. I'd see people leaving because they
couldn't stand the stress of that particular job, and I'd think,
'Give it to me. I could do that. Let me handle the account.'

Eventually I was invited to sit in as an observer on one
meeting with Tiscali, who were complaining that we weren't
matching their IT requirements. I'd been observing the
client/provider relationship for some time and thought I could
see what was going wrong. Basically there was a clash of cul-
tures – each company had their own way of doing things and
their own speed of working, and they didn't always sit com-
fortably together. There wasn't any great issue with what we
did – there just needed to be someone who could understand
why the client wanted certain things and how those could be
best provided by the company. By looking closely at what was
going on, I could see that we could keep them happy if we just
took time to listen properly to their requirements. I wasn't supposed to be contributing at that meeting, but I found I could-
n't stop myself. I introduced myself and told them I worked for
Kingston's IT department. I said that if they told me exactly
what their IT needs were, I'd make sure we delivered a solu-
tion that worked.

They told us; I listened. I knew how the IT department

worked, so I could see in my mind how we could deliver what Tiscali wanted. I knew we could follow their requirements through. I came back from the meeting and prepared a report outlining the situation and proposing solutions to the problems outlined in the meeting and sent it out to all attendees. Tiscali were pleased. Of course I didn't leave it there. Once we'd offered to sort things out, it was important to ensure that everything was running smoothly. They were happy and I ended up building a good relationship with them; things went well and eventually I became the account manager. Everyone has their own strengths – mine is that I can see solutions. It's something that comes naturally to me. But I think the key is to sit and listen first, so that you understand exactly what is required. In general terms, if you understand what your customer wants, you can make sure that is what you deliver; it sounds so simple, but I have been amazed at the number of times it doesn't happen. If you try to force something else on a client you run the risk of sending them to look elsewhere.

By now I was twenty-one years old and I was the account manager of Kingston's biggest client, but still I had the feeling that it wasn't enough. I used to drive down the M62 and look out of the window, see the sign for Hull and think, 'One day I'm going to be doing this on my way out of here. I'm going to see more of the world. This is my home, but there are other places I want to explore and other paths I want to follow. I know life has other things in store for me.' I had a great job and I was settled, but I was frightened that was going to be it. Getting up, going to work, coming home – then doing it all the next day. Until I died. Even though it was a very happy routine, and I had everything that I craved – stability, love, success – it was still a routine and it terrified me.

I bought a house of my own and moved in there. I had a boyfriend at the time, but I wouldn't let him move permanently into my house with me. I wanted a life of my own – I didn't want to be held down by a bloke. I was fiercely independent. There's a Beyoncé song called 'Me, Myself and I'. That's one of the straplines of my life. You need to be able to rely on yourself, because people sometimes let you down. And that's why I wanted my own house. I wanted something that no one was ever going to take away from me.

I'd always dreamed of owning a home of my own. I got a mortgage, but I'd saved enough for a deposit of six thousand pounds and I was able to pay all my own fees. When I babysat for people, I used to ask them not to pay me cash, but to give me things like tea towels and knives and forks for my house. Everything went towards it. I've still got that house now. What I loved most about it was that it was like a fairytale cottage. It had a cobbled, winding path in the garden, leading to the back gate. It was just like the pictures I'd seen in the storybooks I read as a child.

But even the house wasn't enough to banish my feelings of restlessness; I applied for a job in Stoke-on-Trent. I was going to leave Hull and make something of myself. I can't remember where I saw the job advertised, or why I picked Stoke as the place to move to. I was appointed Project Co-ordinator with the Caldwell Group, who are best known for Phones 4U. I was in charge of overseeing the IT delivery for their new stores team. My career plan was to become a project manager, and they knew that when they took me on. The move seemed like a huge step at the time. I looked on Stoke as somewhere where it would all happen. If I'm going to be honest, I think I was channelling all my energy into my career to avoid having to look too deeply at the things that had gone on in my personal life.

I went to Stoke imagining it was all I had ever dreamed of, but of course it was just me and my job. I had the career, but I had no friends, no family, no boyfriend, not even a telephone in my rented flat. I felt completely isolated. It was a low point in my life. But I have a rule about not looking back. If I've made a decision, I stick with it and don't spend time wishing things were different. I'm determined to finish what I've started. That's what kept me in Stoke for nearly a year. But it wasn't easy.

I used to go to the gym at 5 a.m. and throw myself into an exercise routine so there was no time to think about being lonely. No one at work used to go out in the evenings. I was living in a place that was really a house partitioned down the middle, so it was quite a bizarre set-up and I wasn't really happy with it. I'd rented out my own house in Hull. I was determined never to go back at weekends, because I wanted to prove that I could make my decision work. No matter how lonely I got, I was not going to run back and visit friends and family. That would have been too easy. I forced myself to create a life. I'd go shopping, go to the pub on my own, go for dinner on my own. I'd even have Sunday lunch in the pub, sitting by myself. It wasn't easy to make new friends. In some ways it was quite a depressing time, but in many others it was inspirational, because it taught me that it is possible to be self-sufficient. You can go out alone – you don't have to be stuck in night after night just because you're single.

I eventually made a friend at work called Stacey. She was a proper 'Stokie'. She came from Stoke and was very happy. She reminded me a lot of myself as I had been in my earlier days in Hull. She had a nice job, a good car, a nice, easy life and no mad desire to rock the boat. She used to include me in her social life. She's still a good friend, even though I didn't settle down there. So soon I had another decision to make.

CHAPTER FIFTEEN

A Time of Excess

It didn't take long for me to realise that Stoke wasn't where my long-term future lay. Eventually I decided to do something about it. I wasn't going to move back to Hull – I was going to move on. I slipped out of work in my lunch break and used the payphone at ASDA to call a business contact at my old client Tiscali. They'd talked to me before about work in London, but at the time I hadn't been ready to move so far afield. Now I was keen to find out if there might be an opportunity for me.

It so happened that Tiscali were looking into the logistics of moving parts of their business to India. There was a Project Manager vacancy for someone to plan, deliver and oversee the migration – but it would mean being based in London. I drove down for the interview and was offered the job the next day. It all happened so quickly. The day after, I drove down again to look for somewhere to live. Talk about getting off your arse and doing things! I'd never been to London before, so I asked around about how you went about finding accommodation. Someone told me about a paper called *Loot*, so I bought it. I had no idea which part of the city was good and which bad, but Stacey and I rang the numbers in the ads and drove around or got on the tube and went to see a whole load of flats. We saw some of the most awful, hideous sights you can imagine. The experience threw me into a world of different monetary values. People were asking more for a single bedroom in a pokey council flat than I'd been paying for a two-bedroom house up North. Twice as much.

I found a place in Finchley in the end, sharing with three other girls. That was really good fun; it was a lovely house. One of the girls was a nursery teacher, another was a school teacher. I'm not quite sure what the third girl did for a living. We had a good time, a little bit like a family unit. We were all away from home, and we used to cook dinner for each other, sit and watch television together, relax together. On Sundays we'd go down to the local lido and swim for about ten minutes, then we'd go to the local Chinese 'All you can eat' buffet and sit for the whole afternoon, eating. We used to justify it by saying we'd had our swim and we were hungry.

I was quite comfortable, I'd settled into London nicely, and because I was desperate to make friends I wouldn't turn down any invitation. It was the reverse of Stoke. If anyone invited me anywhere, I'd go, so I ended up being out every single night. Before I started work I'd go across the road and have a double-chocolate-chip muffin and an Americano – that was my breakfast every day. I felt so 'London'! We didn't have smart coffee shops in Hull, it was a different world; a different planet. I'd go out to lunch with someone at a bar or café at midday and have a proper meal. Then I'd be out with people from work in the evening and we'd go for dinner or go to the pub and have food. Then I'd feel peckish again on the way home, so I'd go to the Chinese near Oxford Circus tube and have a Chinese takeaway on the tube. London for me was the most exciting place I'd ever seen. I went completely off the rails fashionwise, feeling that I was in this free city where anything goes. I used to experiment like crazy. The stuff I used to wear! I'd do anything to get noticed. I remember having a fluorescent pink string vest with matching fluorescent pink string gloves, of which I only wore one. I'd team them up with combat gear – it was awful! I look back at the pictures and can't believe I ever left home looking like that.

Once I managed to get my housemate and me into the live TV show CD:UK. All the rest of the audience were fourteen- and fifteen-year-olds and there we were, in our twenties, thinking we were really cool. We elbowed the teenagers out of the way and got stuck right next to Cat Deeley, so that when the camera came on, all you could see was me and my housemate. I had a black and white tabard on. At the time, in my mind it looked like high fashion, but with hindsight I looked like a big fat dinner lady. Cat Deeley started saying something about Robbie Williams and I was shouting 'Yaaay!' and lifting my arms in the air. My bingo wings were shaking, all my suet was wobbling and the sight of it on TV was enough to make me cringe when I saw it. When I got off air, I received a text message from a guy I was dating, saying, 'They say the camera adds ten pounds – how many f***ing cameras are you stood in front of? Move, you look awful!'

He was right. I did look awful. Those were fun times, but during those first six months in London I had blossomed to over ten stone, which is the heaviest I've ever been. All those meals out had taken their toll. The consequence was that my bulimia started up in earnest once again. I just felt huge. I decided I had no time to exercise, so I did bulimia instead. Slowly my weight began to drop. As I got thinner, I began to feel that I wanted to exercise again, so before long I was back in the gym at all hours. And this time I took it all one step further. I got hooked on colonic irrigation.

I was addicted. It was like the laxatives only so much more powerful. The purging was a powerful source of cleanliness. Part of the attraction of bulimia for me had always been the idea of being clean; being able to clear your body out so completely was incredible. I can't describe the feeling of satisfaction it gave me. What happens is they put a tube up your bottom and flush litres and litres of water through you. They pump it all out and out comes all your waste. You can see the tube and everything coming out of your body. I felt as though I had discovered the latest, most wonderful process you could imagine. Better even than chocolate laxatives! I loved watching it all happen. If the therapist happened to stand in the way of the apparatus, I'd ask them to move so I could see the entire process. It made me feel so clean, seeing all the waste and bad stuff disappear.

In that first year in London I yo-yo'd from one extreme to another. One minute I was eating nothing but McDonald's, the next I'd be on some uber-healthy diet, when nothing was allowed in my house unless it was good for you. It would be only steamed vegetables, fruit, fish, nothing after certain hours, powder supplements, no dairy, no red meat. My weekly colonics were part of this quest for a healthy lifestyle.

Only I must admit, I did take it a little too far.

My weight dropped to just under seven stone. People began to notice that I was getting too thin. I couldn't see it myself – I still thought I was overweight. Eventually, when I went to a place near where I was living for a colonic, the woman took me to one side and said to me, 'This is not good for my business, what I'm about to do, because I need the money. But have you looked in the mirror recently? You look awful. The second you walked in this building I knew I had to have a chat with you. You're seriously underweight. Your skin is grey. Your cheekbones are painfully protruding. You have black circles under your eyes. Your eyes are bloodshot. You look an absolute mess. What is wrong with you? You don't need colonic irrigation, you need help.'

I was really shocked. She told me to take my clothes off and pulled a mirror in front of me. I stood there, in my underwear.

'What do you see?' she asked me.

'I'm fat,' I said.

She was pointing at all my bones, where they were protruding at the hips. I couldn't see it. I'd psychologically blocked out my own image.

'I look awful,' I sobbed. 'I'm so fat.'

She pushed at my collarbone and pelvis to try to make me

see. It was really hurting, because there was no cushion of fat anywhere, but still I couldn't see it.

I came out and rang my best friend, Vicky.

'She won't treat me,' I sobbed. 'She won't give me the colonic.'

'But you *are* too thin,' she said. 'The woman's right. You do look awful, Michelle. Not because you're overweight, but because you're underweight.'

I refused to believe her. I walked up the road to a different clinic and booked an appointment under a different name. I didn't mention anything about what had just happened. Afterwards, I rang up the woman who'd refused to treat me and told her about it. She warned me again to stop doing it. She said my blood pressure was so low that I was putting myself in danger. For once, I decided to listen.

I'm not sure you ever really get rid of bulimia, which seems to be a common complaint now. I think you learn to manage it. To my mind it's not an illness you can be cured of; I think it's an urge, an addiction, and you have to understand what's causing it. When you're suffering from it, you don't see your bulimia as something bad; it's your saving grace. You can eat whatever you want, have the taste of whatever you want to taste and then you can get rid of it. I know that's deluded. It's certainly not what I believe now, but I saw it that way at the time and I imagine it's what many, many bulimics think.

These days, if I have two McDonald's in a day, I say to myself, 'Right, Michelle, if you do this you have to deal with the consequences. You'll have to deal with the way it feels having two McDonald's in your stomach. Do you want to do that?'

When I was recovering I would make it clear to myself that if I wanted to eat too much junk food, then I would have to live with it − it wasn't a case of, 'Oh, I'll indulge myself and then I can throw up, so it won't matter.' That wasn't an option any more. I still do my best to eat as healthily as I want to, but I am often tempted by junk food and takeaways − they're easy when you live alone and have a busy schedule. However, I try to fill my fridge with healthy foods instead. There's no two ways about it. I've learnt that anorexia, bulimia and extreme diets are not the way to a healthy lifestyle and a good body shape. The best way to stay well is to eat the right foods and keep yourself moving: eat healthily and exercise.

I can say these things with hindsight, but it was a long struggle to get to the point where I recognise them and acknowledge it's how I want to live my life. At the period when my bulimia started, my self-image was badly distorted. When I looked in the mirror I saw someone fat. I think the most important thing is to understand the reasons why you're bulimic. What is it that's driving you to do it? Ask yourself why you're throwing up. Is it because you're eating junk food? If so, *why* are you eating all this junk food? What is it that's making you do that? If you go out and eat a lot of rubbish, then chances are it will make you feel pretty sick. Are you so unhappy that you're comfort eating? Or are you putting junk in because you see yourself as worthless? If you're eating normally, but are still bulimic, why is that? You feel fat, you have low self-esteem − but why? I think bulimia isn't the root problem; it's a symptom of something else. It's an action we take because of an underlying problem. Now that I'm a bit older and wiser I can see that we have a blueprint inside us that's like an emotional DNA. It's like a computer program in our mind that controls how we think about things and react to things. I've realised that we have to reprogram that blueprint the way we want it. I think bulimia is the symptom, not the cause.

After around a year, I moved out of the shared house. I wanted more out of London life. I wanted to experience things I'd never experienced before. Once again I was thinking, 'What if I die? I'm not doing the London thing. I've failed to live up to my plan.'

For some reason I decided to relocate south of the river. I've no idea why – I think someone must have told me the area was a trendy place to live. I started looking and one day thought I'd hit the jackpot. I went down one Sunday to look round this house – and it was stunning. There was a big group of housemates in the lounge, all with their pyjamas on, with fairy lights and candles lit, watching a film together. I thought, 'Wow, this looks amazing!' I moved in a couple of days later.

It wasn't what I'd hoped for. I didn't feel that I really fitted in, but at first I wasn't sure why. The others were a lot older than me, mainly Aussies and Kiwis. They were all very nice, hard-working people. Some had senior jobs in banking. There was lots of money around and they were out to enjoy the London lifestyle. Just what I'd wanted. Only it didn't feel quite right. Downstairs was the lounge and the kitchen, which was the focal point of the house. They'd have their friends round and people used to sit on the big pine bench and others would cook. It was a family atmosphere, but I wasn't really part of it. Somehow I felt on the outside.

I suspected after a while that they were into drugs. It became crystal clear one weekend when we were all in the lounge together watching a film. There was a knock on the door, and someone got up to open it. Before I knew what was happening, a scruffy guy had come in, wearing a bum bag, and was asking people what they wanted. He was taking drugs orders – so many cokes, so many Es, so much of this, so much of that. He got to me and said, 'What's your order?' and I said, 'Well, there isn't one, thanks.' He left, but I was thinking, 'Shit, this isn't really going to work. I've got to get out of here.'

I didn't socialise with them much, because I didn't want to be involved in that kind of scene. It was difficult to avoid them completely, though. On one occasion they threw a big party. I invited a couple of my work friends, but I should have known better. On one end of the big kitchen table there was a big pile of coke, on the other a big pile of Es – and there were my workmates. I was mortified. I made my excuses and shoved my mates out of the door, apologising and telling them that I'd had no idea it was going to be that kind of party. We went to a local pub instead, and when I came back I locked my door and went to bed.

I knew I wanted to move out but couldn't think what to do because I had nowhere to go immediately. When I'd realised that the housemates were into drugs, I'd talked to three girls at work and we'd agreed that we would move in together in a few months' time. They were tied up in a letting contract and I'd agreed to put up with where I was until they were free. Now I just wanted to leave quickly. I looked on the website at work and found a room that sounded ideal. It was no hassle, no contract, cash in hand. It would tide me over until I could move in with my friends.

Of course it was too good to be true. It turned out to be a squat. The owner of the house had tried to kick the tenants out, because he wanted to turn it into flats and rent it for more money. The tenants had refused to go and had started sub-letting the rooms instead. The house was absolutely huge. They showed me to what would be my room and it was awful. The ceiling was black with damp; so were the walls. Someone had stuck up an enormous map of the world to cover up the damp patches. In the kitchen, the fridge was coated with slime and water. It stank. The bottom of the bath was covered with a layer of slime, mildew and stinking water because there was no extractor fan. But I was so desperate to get out of where I was that I took it.

I resigned myself to the fact that I was never going to shower in that house. I wasn't going to brush my teeth in the sink or eat a meal in that property or sit in the lounge. Every morning I used to get up early, go to the gym, shower, clean my teeth and get ready for work there. I went out every night. Never once did I eat a meal in that flat. I sat in the lounge once, when I'd come in a bit too tipsy to really care. Even helped by alcohol it was awful. They were smoking and burning the furniture. I don't know how many people were living there, and I never found out who they all were. I stayed there a couple of months, all the while reminding myself it was a means to an end, and then the girls' contracts came to an end and we all moved in to Lavender Hill. It felt like paradise.

CHAPTER SIXTEEN

Achieving Success

My job at Tiscali was Migrations Manager. They were relocating some of their UK operation to India – this is known as off-shore outsourcing. Companies outsource abroad for many reasons ranging from cost saving to time efficiencies. Tiscali were migrating quite a large percentage of their operations to India and my job was to scope, plan, manage and deliver the migrations. This included the recruitment, training and redundancies.

Tiscali had their own reasons for outsourcing some of their operation at that time, but in general it's a process that many UK firms consider at some point. Competition is rife in the current economy, and lots of companies need to cut costs. If a business is slow on the uptake, they may find their competitors have taken steps already and they're being priced out of the market. The important thing is to think ahead. Moving an operation to a cheaper labour source, such as India, can sometimes mean the difference between survival and collapse.

In general terms, the benefits of outsourcing go beyond cost-cutting to increased efficiency if it's handled right. For example, if you work for a UK-based operator you may have a document from a client come in at 5 p.m. on a Friday. You want to process it, but everyone's going home. If you start to process it first thing on Monday morning, your client has to wait for the answer until Monday afternoon. If you work with somewhere like India, you could find your answer waiting for you first thing on Monday – or on Saturday, if you chose to go in then. The time difference works in your favour, giving a 'follow the sun' type benefit; and the job structure is very different overseas, giving you a more motivated workforce. In a UK call centre you might have staff who are looking on it as a transient position before they move on to something better or a more convenient job. In India you tend to have high-calibre graduates who really want to work in those call centres and who approach the job with a great deal of pride.

My new role at Tiscali really appealed to me. The work was great. I thoroughly enjoyed it and got to travel to India a lot. I knew I was playing a major part in something that was vital to Tiscali's profitable future. Efficiency in business is something that is crucial, and at that point I was at the cutting edge of a move to create a highly cost-effective operation.

I'll never forget the first time I went to India. I was travelling in a senior capacity on business and it was very exciting. It was the first time I'd flown anywhere on my own; when I'd travelled before it had been on holiday to places like Benidorm and Ibiza, always with friends. When I stepped off the plane in Goa, where I had an overnight stop, I was absolutely overwhelmed. I didn't really know what was supposed to happen, or what the immediate plan was. There were hundreds of men in brown coats at the airport – they were porters, although I didn't realise it right away. A crowd of them started grabbing my bags and pushing and pulling them around and taking them over to the other side of the concourse. I wasn't sure what was going on and tried to regain control of my bag – it was completely bewildering.

Before I knew it, I was in the back of a taxi. I'd managed to tell the driver the name of the hotel I was staying in, and he'd seemed to recognise it, so I hoped he was going to take me there. I was absolutely terrified. The driver fancied himself as a bit of a Nigel Mansell, but the roads we were on weren't much more than dirt tracks. There seemed no concept of the Highway Code or road safety at all; everyone was driving everywhere. We had no seat belts, and were careering in and out of bumps and potholes along dusty streets with Indian music blaring full blast out of the radio and religious ornaments dangling off all the mirrors. My driver was singing away and chanting as he dodged in and out of the traffic and I was just thinking, 'Oh my God, what have I got myself into?' There were massive cows all over the streets. Cows are holy animals in India and the drivers won't hassle them, let alone run them over, so when a cow steps out, you just have to wait until it feels like moving over, because you'd never hit one. There were also goats and chickens and all sorts wandering round among them, right in the middle of the street – it was chaos.

We turned off down a side road and into an area that was well off the beaten track. I started wondering if the taxi driver was planning on taking me away somewhere and doing something to me. We were passing whole families of people out on the street. Tiny little kids with no clothes on would surge up to the windows and knock on them, holding their hands out and begging. I was so upset I started to cry. I could see all these makeshift places where people lived; no more than huts, really, with nothing inside them. They had nothing. Absolutely nothing.

Finally we turned back onto the main track. It was absolute bedlam. A bus would go by with about two hundred people on, even though it was made for no more than fifty. There would be passengers on the roof racks, hanging off the back, wherever they could get a foot- or a handhold. Then you'd see a moped go by with an entire family on it. There'd be a man driving, a woman on the back, a child perched on the seat between them, a baby in the woman's arms and another one on her back. It was another world.

I actually found the whole situation quite scary. I remember ringing one of the managers at Tiscali and crying down the phone. Then we pulled up at the hotel. Suddenly, everything seemed a lot better. I started to think, 'Well, this is OK. I'm suddenly soothed.' It was a five-star hotel in the middle of nowhere. It was lovely. I went to the room and had a meal. I ordered a hamburger. God knows what was in it, but it certainly wasn't beef. I still don't know what they'd killed to make it, but no way was I going to eat it. The chips were a safe bet, though. I was out there for a few weeks and I lived off chips.

Tiscali were setting up a contact centre out in Bangalore. My job was to oversee the setting up of the centre, meet the suppliers and make sure all the technology was in place and working. I had to make sure the project was progressing according to plan, check that they were employing the right people, ensure that the layout was right and that the contracts were all in place.

My work has taken me to India a few times, and, after the initial shock, I really got to like it out there, and grew to appreciate the Indian culture. Our clients would take us out to the very expensive places to eat, and there was another manager out in Bangalore, whose staff I got to know quite well. We used to go out to the trendy bars and had some great fun evenings.

India's got two sides at different extremes. You've either got the very, very poor or the very rich; there didn't seem to me to be any middle ground. In the end, you became hardened, to some extent, to the poverty around you. Initially, I used to give money to everyone I could, but then I realised I couldn't help all of them. Hard as it was, I tried to stop being affected by it quite so much. I do find the disparity between the two sides distressing, though. I wish I could do more to help the poor people there, but the country is so big and such a different world from the one I'm used to. There are a lot of smart, educated people in India, and if they can't see a way to sort out the way things are, how can I solve the problems during a three-week visit? When you go there, you have to accept what you see and get on and do the job you've been sent to do.

When I was working at Tiscali, even though I now had a successful career, I was starting to feel restless. Once again I could see I was getting into a routine. Getting up, going to work, going home. Up the next morning to repeat the pattern. I was thinking, 'What if you die before you've travelled the world?' In the end I couldn't ignore it any longer. It became my ambition to travel, and I began to form plans. I started spending every lunchtime in the Karrimor world travel shop. I'd go for backpack fittings. The bloke who worked in there would try different types of rucksack on me, with weights in the various pockets to see how they felt. We'd talk for hours about his experiences; where he'd travelled and so on. I started buying all the gadgets, like towels that fit into a space the size of a ten pence piece and safety door locks; and Lonely Planet guides. On the Lonely Planet site there's a forum called the Thorn Tree, which I used to browse all the time. It's an online community where you can look things up and chat to other travellers – it was amazing. I worked out my trip. It was going to take in New Zealand, Australia, Thailand – I was going to see the world. I made contact with other people who were going to be out there at the same time as me. I made lists. I visualised my goals. I got really excited. I handed in my notice at work.

Then one day, I said to myself, 'Hang about. This isn't you, you're a career girl. Why do you want to throw everything away – all the stuff you worked for – to go travelling with a backpack for a year? Why are you doing it?' I had a bit of a reality check and realised that it wasn't what I wanted to do at all, I just felt like I should. I started thinking, 'Sod that! My life is business. I want to be back in business. I can see the world bit by bit, and I don't need to take a year out.'

I'm not proud. I don't mind admitting when I've made a mistake. I went back to my manager saying I'd changed my mind. Could I go back to my old job? By then I'd already worked my notice and they'd made arrangements.

My manager said, 'You're posing me a bit of a problem. I don't want to lose you, Michelle, but we've already restructured everything. We've appointed your replacement. We can't go back on our offer to them – it's all in writing. But we do like you and we do think you're good at your job. We can take you back in a different capacity.'

The new position was something to do with process engineering. It was great that I was back in the land of business again, but not so great that I was lined up with something I didn't really want to do. I started thinking. I had been really good at the liaison work with India. If Tiscali wanted to outsource, there must be many more businesses out there wanting to outsource too. Why not do something on my own?

I did some research. I had a contact called Gill, who was a contractor who had also worked for Tiscali. I had met her some years before and used to want to be like her – she was working for herself, earning a lot of money per day, doing really well. What was stopping me from doing what she was doing? I had plenty of skills going for me. I started digging around, doing my homework and finding out all I could about freelance work. How much could I earn? How would I go about it? I was very excited about the prospect of being self-employed and decided to go it alone.

I applied for a freelance contract as a programme manager with a major telecoms company. They wanted someone to manage the captive offshoring process for their whole technology division. I would lead transitions which would impact on hundreds of people in a lot of different departments, and I would be working with the board level senior directors on restructuring the company. On the first day I found I was really nervous. The director had gone to a lot of trouble to think about our department and what we'd need. She'd done a really good job of sorting our day out, making sure we had laptops available and so on – it was brilliantly organised. It was obvious that the company was taking the offshoring programme very seriously and had invested a lot of money in getting the operation set up. I was so proud to be part of it.

We were a team of eight. I remember doing a 'round robin' with the rest of the team that day, where we all introduced ourselves and spoke about what we did. Each of the programme managers talked about how many degrees they had and I just sat there thinking, 'Shit, I haven't got any! How am I going to explain this away?' I decided just to be honest and open and explained that I had worked my way up in business rather than going to university. I shouldn't have worried; everyone accepted me just fine.

Although the others were much older than me and therefore by default had more experience, I was probably the most qualified to do the job we were actually doing. I was the only person who had experience of India, and the only one who had a background in offshoring, redundancies, re-engineering or any of the processes involved. I had the two biggest divisions to manage – two separate technology divisions, each one having many sub-departments. Combined, they represented a very large percentage of the overall company. I was the youngest person, with the least experience as a programme manager, and I had a big challenge, because the workforce was very resistant to the whole idea of outsourcing to India. When they saw me on that first day, I think they breathed a sigh of relief and thought, 'Young blonde girl, great, nothing's ever going to happen.' They expected me to be a little timid girl, and believed that they would be able to get away with anything. I'm sure that some believed that none of them would have to go to India because this girl couldn't possibly be capable of making it happen. Little did they know, as they went home that day, how wrong they were.

Offshoring or outsourcing projects are generally sensitive matters within an organisation. Such business change is often viewed by staff as a threat because unfortunately there can inevitably be some element of staff redundancy or job restructuring. To make a success of such a programme, it is important that the companies are as honest and open to their staff as possible while at the same time trying to reduce the impact of the change. To get the best results, you need to get the staff on board and behind the projects as much as is possible.

I planned hard for my first meeting with the managers and outlined exactly who I was and what I was about. After listening to their thoughts and concerns, I explained what the main directors were trying to achieve and how we had decided it would happen, and I stressed how important it was that they bought into the whole idea. Ultimately, people need to understand that companies have to evolve constantly to meet market demands – if the workforce is too resistant to change it may mean everyone's jobs going under. Often the main reason for outsourcing is a company's bottom line. Coming in from outside as a freelance enabled me to take the tough stance that was necessary. If you're detached, you can have a clearer view of the overall picture. However sympathetic I might feel, I still had to tell people that if they stood against the evaluation process, it wasn't going to help because a decision had already been taken that it was going to happen, with or without their support.

I spent time making sure each individual understood what outsourcing to India meant to them personally, and what the plus sides could be to them. For some, it could present exciting new opportunities. They could choose to co-operate and get the best possible deal, new experience or relocation for themselves, or they could dig in their heels and risk losing everything. It was very hard to start with. Key staff would fail to turn up to meetings. When they did, they'd just sit there and insist that nothing they did could go out to India. They'd spend ages explaining to me how all the work in their department absolutely had to stay in England. That meant I'd have to dig around and investigate their reasoning, then show them that it was based on a false premise.

The argument would run, 'We need to stay in England because we use this bit of paper and it has to be kept here because it's needed by the team next door who have to work with us.'

I'd say, 'Let me get this straight. You're team A and you need to be here because you interact with team B who are also here. OK. How about we offshore both teams?'

They used to get angry, I'm sure, but they didn't do it to my face. I used to hold regular video conference meetings. I'd get India, UK, Belgium and France linked up. I'd lay out the project plans and explain exactly what was expected of everyone and what they were required to do, when they were expected to do it and how. I made sure everyone knew what they were doing at all times. My projects were like my babies. I understood them inside and out and I was determined that each of them would succeed. Over time, my project teams began to trust me and I began to trust them. I managed to get everyone on board. I developed a really good relationship with the two senior directors. They backed me, and got to the point where they really trusted my decisions. If I said they would need to make ten people redundant in this area, they'd trust my opinion. I felt they understood that I knew what I was doing.

Then the company appointed a new managing director for 'Transformation' – restructuring the company. She didn't want the Indian operation to have a separate identity, she wanted it to be integrated with the rest of the company, so she finished the whole programme we were working on and disbanded it. All the contracts were ended, and the one permanent member of staff, the director for India, was made redundant. Then they called me to a meeting. They said they were highly impressed with me, and, while they were terminating the other contracts, they would like to extend mine for another year and give me a big pay rise. The director said she was very pleased with the results I'd achieved and wanted me to teach the rest of the business how to get the kinds of results that my divisions had. She wanted to apply my techniques throughout the company.

I spent several months doing this. Then they offered me a permanent job. It brought me to another crossroads. Did I *want* a permanent job? What else was there to achieve? Should I be out there doing something more, chasing other goals?

It was at this point that someone put the application form for *The Apprentice* under my nose, and I thought, 'Great. What a wonderful, exciting opportunity.' I was thrilled by the prospect of having a successful mentor, of experiencing a different side to business, and intrigued by the TV element.

So I filled it in.

Eight years earlier, I'd been a drunk, depressed, suicidal teenager with two GCSE passes, going firmly off the rails. What little self-confidence I had was being constantly undermined by domestic violence. I'd come a long way since then. I'd transformed myself into a sought-after high-flyer earning a six-figure salary. I owned two properties: one in Hull, another in London. I'd bought my own car, plus a Vespa scooter as a runaround. I'd worked in London and abroad. I had a thriving social life with a wide circle of friends. I shopped in designer boutiques, ate in the best restaurants and I drank champagne whenever I felt like it, in trendy London bars. I had one business credit card which was always paid off in full, and owed nothing apart from my modest mortgage. How had I turned myself around?

I suppose one of the most important things was having a goal to focus on. I realised that it's easy to get trapped in a vicious circle. If you don't know where you want to be, you're never going to get there. If you haven't got the right paper qualifications, you might find yourself in a job you don't like or a career that's going nowhere, but because you need the money, it seems like you have no choice. Getting the YTS place with St John Ambulance helped me to get out of my own personal rut, but I did have to take a drop in my take-home pay in order to do it. If I hadn't had a goal in mind, there wouldn't have been the incentive to do the training on low pay, or to gain the necessary qualifications in my spare time. Forming that career plan was crucial.

One of the reasons I'm telling my story is because I want people to see that if they are stuck in a rut or a job they're not happy with, they don't need to stay there just because they've ended up there through force of circumstances. It is possible to change the course of your life as I did, but you have to set yourself goals and you have to have the determination to see it through. There's a tendency to think you have just the one chance at school or college, and if you don't fit into the education system as a kid, well, too bad. But that's not right. Not everyone is suited to the conventional path of school, college and career – and I feel very strongly that people should not write themselves off just because they weren't academic.

I've already spent time talking to schools about business, and I'm determined to do more to help kids make more of their lives, particularly if they don't have a very good start or aren't getting on so well at studying. My youngest brother Paul, for example, isn't very academic, but I'm confident that he's going to be a great achiever. Since the age of about seven he's shown business acumen. He recognised that he could go to Kwik Save and buy six doughnuts for 50p, then go to school and sell them for 30p each. The kids like the doughnuts and he does well out of it. He's always trading. I keep telling my mum to harness what he's got and develop it, rather than try to stamp it out.

I think that often the problem with schools is that there's only one way of doing things, and that's their way. I won't deny that academic qualifications do help, and for many roles they are essential – I chose to study for mine in my own time, after all. They give you the theory to complement your practice, which I think is important – but it's very wrong to say you have to be *either* academic *or* practical to achieve. It's the combination of common sense, hands-on experience and study that makes for success. If a child like my brother can do something like sell doughnuts, then it's not right to stop him just because it might be a bit inconvenient within the system. If an eleven-year-old child can recognise off his own bat that he can undercut the school tuck shop, then to me that's a sign of business genius. Practical talents that will help in the outside world should be encouraged and not brushed aside. School is great, but it's an education that's important. I might not have done well at school, but I educated myself in other ways and am well on track to making a success of my life.

CHAPTER SEVENTEEN

Auditions

I love striving to achieve my best. Occasionally I gather friends and colleagues together for group sessions where we can bounce ideas off each other. It was one of these ad hoc gatherings that started me off along the path towards the next phase of my career. I'd mustered a number of us for an informal discussion meeting to analyse where our lives were going. There were a good few of us taking part in that particular session. One of them, a guy called Andrew, said to me, 'Do you know what, Michelle, I've got an idea for what you should do next, and it's something you'd be brilliant at. It's a TV show.' He started telling me about *The Apprentice*, which had started in the United States with Donald Trump as the adjudicating businessman and had now completed a successful first series in the UK with Sir Alan Sugar in the main hiring and firing role.

My first reaction was, 'Wow, I've always wanted a successful mentor.' I knew that Sir Alan Sugar was a top businessman of iconic status, and I could think of no better mentor to have.

Even though the salary was less than I was earning, I was willing to take the drop because of the opportunities to be mentored. I thought, 'If you don't try, you'll never know' so I decided to go for it.

I took the application form home. It was about twelve pages long and I decided I couldn't be bothered to fill it in right away. I left it for later, as you do, and forgot about it. I was tidying up one day when I came across it again. That day happened to be the closing date. It was too late to post it and I didn't have a PC at home at the time, so I couldn't sit down to fill it in online. For a moment I wasn't sure whether to throw it away or take the trouble to fill it in. It would have been really easy for me to think, 'I can't be bothered,' or, 'I'll never get picked,' but I decided I was going to make the effort to go to the Internet café down the road to take the first step. Incidentally, that's one of the top tips I always emphasise when I'm giving business talks: *taking the first step*. Getting yourself started is often the most difficult part of any process. Anyway, I logged on and filled in the form, little imagining how it would change the course of my life.

It was a long, detailed process, and quite a difficult task. On the one hand I tried to be as honest as possible in answering the questions; on the other hand, it was an application form and I was trying to consider what they wanted from their candidates. What was the best way of presenting myself? Should I emphasise my serious side, or try to be funny or unusual? What would catch their eye and put me above the other entrants? In the end I just decided to be me. Once I'd filled in what I could, I sent it off and didn't really expect to hear anything back, but

I was happy because I'd made the effort to do it and wouldn't look back and regret a wasted opportunity.

A couple of days later I was surprised to receive an email, offering me an audition. Being the kind of person I am, I was on the phone to my circle of friends right away, telling them about it and asking what they thought my chances were. My family's reaction was along the lines of, 'Yeah, whatever, Michelle,' because I was always ringing them up with exciting ideas for projects I intended to get involved in, and some of them happened and some of them didn't.

My mum had got used to me coming up with what she thinks of as hare-brained schemes. I used to call her up and say something like, 'Today, my life's changed. I've realised that my future is in coffee shops. I'm going to open the first coffee shop in Hull, get a manager to run it and that'll be my future.' And she'd learned to say, 'Right, OK.' She'd know that the next week I might be ringing and telling her something like, 'I'm going to open a yoga retreat. I'm going to be a yoga teacher. I'm going to change people's lives and it's all going to be good.' So when I phoned and said I was auditioning for a TV show, and I was going to apply for a job and hopefully get it and work for Sir Alan Sugar, they imagined it was just another of those things. I started teasing my brothers and saying, 'I'm going to be a famous businesswoman and go on TV,' but they just laughed and said, 'Whatever.'

The audition was being held in a really swanky hotel in London. I remember getting on my moped and setting off, weaving through the streets and pulling up outside. I was about an hour late. I got off the bike and saw a big flip chart outside

saying: *Apprentice Auditions. Queue this way*. I remember thinking, 'Eugh, this is just like *Big Brother* – what am I doing?' And
instantly, that little voice of doubt in my head started saying,
'What are *you* doing here? Who's going to pick *you*? You don't
belong here. What have you got to offer TV land? Who's going
to offer *you* a job?'

I pushed those thoughts to the back of my head and considered what to do next. As I was running late, I decided I
would walk into the hotel and pretend that I wasn't part of *The
Apprentice* but only a guest, so that I could evaluate the situation and see what was going on. That was my way of getting
myself to take the first step. So I walked into the foyer, and I
was just overwhelmed. There were what looked like thousands
of young wannabe business people. Some looked daft and
crazy, wearing all kinds of weird and wonderful things; some
were loud and leery; there were some quiet studenty types,
people sitting with their *Apprentice* books in the corner, lots of
people carrying Alan Sugar articles and Amstrad financial
reports. I just stared, thinking, '*Oh my God.*' Everyone else
seemed really confident. I just thought, 'Bollocks to that' and
walked straight out again.

I rang my friend Vicky and said, 'How about we go for a
coffee? I've changed my mind about this audition.'

She said, 'No, I'm not coming for a coffee. You get yourself
back in there and stop being silly.'

I went back in and I almost made it all the way up to the
reception desk to say I'd come for *The Apprentice*, but in the
end I backed out. I sat on my moped and rang another friend
and suggested we go for lunch.

He said, 'Look, this is a one-off opportunity. Why don't you do it just for the experience? So you can say you've done a TV audition. If nothing else, it will be a great pub story.'

No one suggested I was actually going to get through. They just suggested I should take part in the audition and make the most of the experience. In the end I went back in again. I was so nervous, my knees were actually shaking. I had to go right up to the front and say who I was. The woman didn't even look at me, she just looked at the paper and said I was an hour late for my session. She told me that I'd have to wait and they'd see me when they could fit me in.

I sat in the waiting room with all the others, listening to them bleating on about how much money they earned, how many companies they had, how successful they were, how they were going to win and how they were so excited about it. I sat there quietly making small talk with a few people and sharing another contestant's chocolate muffins. I'd lost the impulse to walk out by then. There were a whole load of people coming in and going out; it was just like the old Scooby-Doo cartoons when Shaggy and Scooby are running down a corridor – past the clock, past the chair, past the clock again – and never getting anywhere. And here we all were with people going out and in, out and in, and we weren't really moving.

Five hours later I got called for my interview. It turned out to be really easy. They just asked me a few questions, I answered them, and I was through to the next round. There was a bench outside and you either got sent to sit on the bench for the next interview, or you went home. When I was called into the next room for the second audition, it was another one-on-one interview, and again I got through. Some of them were similar questions to those you might be asked in any job interview. There were so many people hanging around. I've never seen so many crowded together, except at a football match or something like that.

All of a sudden it got tougher. I got called through again and asked to sit with a group and it was scary. One girl was talking non-stop. I imagine she was probably just nervous or insecure, but she was going on and on about how she wanted to make a film called *From Smack to Crack*. Then she was going to make a sequel called *And Back*. It was just awful. Everyone else seemed to be in hysterics. I just sat there thinking, 'You're not even funny, and I actually find what you're talking about quite insulting.'

I thought, 'I'm not going to get on very far here. I'm not prepared to start laughing at something that isn't amusing just because everyone else is. I don't think it's funny and I can't pretend that it is.' I felt quite different from the rest of the gang. One of the guys was going on about his offices in Berkeley Square and his share portfolio and his hedge fund and his car. My instinct said, 'What a tosser.' But another part of me was saying, 'He's got all this stuff – I haven't got anything like that.'

Another girl was saying how she'd founded one of the biggest recruitment agencies in London, which had been named after her and which we were all supposed to have heard of. So I was thinking, 'Fuck. What have I done? I haven't done much, really.' Of course, with hindsight, I can see that I'd probably achieved a lot more in real terms than many of those people in there, but I couldn't see it right then.

We got called into a big meeting room. We were asked, 'Who is the best businessman out of all these people on the board?'

Instantly everyone started talking. They were all trying to get themselves recognised by the panel, saying, 'I think this, what about that, well, I believe this ...'

I just sat there. I felt like I was shrinking into the background. I was thinking, 'Do something. Say something. Because if you don't do something or say something in the next few minutes then you're going home.' It wasn't necessarily that I wanted to be on the TV show, it was more about wanting to prove a point. I wanted to prove something, to make my mark.

Eventually I said very quietly, 'Excuse me ... Hello ... ?'

They all looked at me as if to say, 'And who the fuck are you?'

I said, 'Listen, guys, this is really quite simple, in my opinion. We might already have the answer. All of you are wanting your say, which is quite understandable as you all want to be noticed by the panel, but how about we stop, take stock, start again, and do a quick round robin to see what everyone's choices are. It might be that we've already got the answer, without having to create a debate. Let's start with me. My choice is X.'

I then pointed at the person next to me. 'Say what your choice is. You don't have to say why, at this point. Just choose one, so we can speedily go round and see where we stand.' We went round the table and it turned out we had a consensus of opinion. Everyone had chosen the same man, except for one person.

'Right, guys,' I said. 'It's very clear we've got an answer

already. I therefore don't feel that there's any need for further debate. We don't need to waste anyone's time; we should put our answer to the panel and then go. Does everyone agree?'

They all said yes. I told the judges who we'd chosen – and then we left. '

I was the first to be called through out of that group into another room for a further chat. Then we sat back down for a bit until I was called through to do a screen test. It makes me cringe every time I see it. It's been on the BBC website and I think my hair and eyes look terrible. I had to talk to the camera and say, 'My name's Michelle, I'm from Hull and I'm looking forward to *The Apprentice* because of X.' Quite simple stuff, no rocket science.

After that I just left. I remember thinking, 'Crikey, I found that quite easy.' After I'd got on to the programme, I found out why they'd picked me. I was told that it was because when I was in the group sessions, I spoke and everybody stopped and listened and that what I said was clear, concise and very, very relevant.

For the next stage there were loads of us in the group, and once again my initial feeling was one of slight intimidation. Jo and Ansell, who ended up going through with me, were in this group. When I first met Jo, I was absolutely overwhelmed by her. She had such a loud laugh and so much hair. Everyone sat round a big, rectangular table with name badges on. I'd been caught in the rain with my crash helmet on, so below the line of the helmet my hair was all wet and curly, while I had a perfect helmet shape welded into the hair on top. I was mortified because I looked so hideous.

To start with we were given a subject to debate. Well, cue mayhem is all I can say about that. Instantly, all these people, desperate and determined to be noticed, started to speak. Everyone wanted to be heard; everyone wanted to be right; everyone tried to make sure the producers recognised them – it was boardroom carnage. You couldn't understand anybody. I just shrank further and further away because I hate that kind of behaviour. Eventually I thought, once again, 'Dewberry, you've got to say something or go home. And you haven't driven all this way with dodgy hair just to leave without saying anything; so speak.'

I said, in a small but confident voice, 'Guys ... excuse me ...'

At that, Jo took a deep breath and yelled: 'Excuse me!! Michelle wants ... to ... speak!!! And I think we should listen to what she has to say!'

Everyone's attention swivelled on to me. I thought, 'Shit, I'd better make it something interesting, then.' I said, 'Guys. Commendable enthusiasm here. But I can't hear anybody. I can't understand a word that's being said – or shouted, as is probably more appropriate. What I think we need to do is have a bit of structure, or we're not going to achieve what we're meant to achieve and the time's going to run out. So here's what I propose. We need to structure this and every debate going forward with a simple set of rules. We need a chairperson. That chairperson is to be solely responsible for the direction the debate goes in. That chairperson has the final say on anything. If you want to speak, you put your hand up and the chairperson will point at whoever he or she thinks should take the floor at that moment. If you want to go next, raise your hand, get the chair's acknowledgement, wait for the person speaking to finish and then have your say. This way every person round the table will get a fair say, because it's obviously very important that we all get a chance to contribute to the discussion, that everyone's point of view gets heard, and everyone gets the opportunity to put forward their points and reach an agreement on what we're here to do.'

The whole atmosphere in the room changed. I said, 'Right, who wants to be chairperson then?' and some smart Alec said, 'I think you should because it was your idea.' I'd never really chaired a debate before, but I thought that it couldn't be that hard. I said what the agenda was and asked who wanted to start, then launched in, picking someone and asking what the point they wanted to make was.

Someone would get going, then another person would chime in with, 'Oh, I don't think that's a valid point.' I was firm. I told them that whether it was valid or not was irrelevant, because we were getting ideas out onto the table, not closing them down or shutting them off. I was quite in control. I appointed a time-keeper to keep track of the debate so we didn't overrun. And from that point on in the day, every single discussion we had in the group took the same format. I felt quite proud of myself. I don't think it's anything special. As I said, it comes naturally to me, but it's something anybody could do. Only no one else had thought of doing it.

As we went on, each successive chairperson got stronger as they understood what the role was about. I think it was brilliant that everyone picked up on it and improved their performance. A small part of me was disappointed because I thought, 'Oh, I wasn't as good a chairperson as him.' But then I thought, 'Nonsense. I created the concept. Those people have learned from watching what's going on. I got the ball rolling; I'm every bit as good as them.'

My way is to sit and listen. But when I do speak, I make sure that what I have to say is valuable and relevant. In my last job before *The Apprentice*, my director said that I used to sit in meetings and not say much – but when I did speak it was genius. I was informed, because I'd listened to what other people had said; considered because I'd thought about their points and taken them on board; rational, sensible and very clear. I might not be loud or forceful, but I don't let people bully me. I could be at a boardroom table at our weekly project meetings and someone would try to summarise what I thought, but I'd say, 'I'm sorry, that's not what I'm saying, what I'm saying is this. Don't try and tell me I'm saying something else. You're doing it because you aren't listening to me and the reason you're not listening is because you keep repeating your own views without hearing anyone else's.' One of my strengths is my ability to communicate in a really clear and concise way.

Once *The Apprentice* auditions got going I wasn't particularly aware of the competition element. I did realise I had to be noticed, but I didn't think it had to be to anyone else's detriment. I didn't feel the need to shout over anybody or steal someone's ideas or pretend I was better than the others. I just needed to be me. It was like any other work situation. When people have been in a meeting with me, I like them to walk away and think, 'Oh yes, she was good. She knew what she was talking about and added value.' But that's in all situations. The audition was no different, as far as that was concerned.

When the call came from the team at Talkback to tell me I'd got through, all I can remember thinking is '*Really*?' in a surprised, semi-disbelieving kind of way. I was just leaving my flat when the phone rang, and I'd had to run upstairs to answer it. My mind was on other things, and I was a little bit blasé about it, I suppose. I don't think I comprehended just how big it was going to be and how much it was going to change my life. It was only when I started getting the emails telling me details of what was going to happen and setting out the rules of the competition that I started to think, 'Bloody hell, this is quite something.'

I was excited, naturally, but I just carried on with my life for the weeks before filming began. I did tell my family and closest friends – it would have been impossible to disappear off to *The Apprentice* house for up to two months without saying anything to anyone – but they were sworn to secrecy and we were all really careful. I didn't do a single ounce of preparation and I hadn't watched the first series anyway. I had decided I was just going to be me – and you can't prep for being your-self, can you? I didn't have a clue what to expect; I just thought it would be a great experience. I have quite a static excitement level. It takes a huge amount to actually break through this and for me to show it. So I thought, 'Oh, that's nice. It'll give me something to do for the next few months. Hopefully, I'll have a great time along the way and end up with a mentor.' And that was literally all it was. Because I'd won, lots of applicants for the third series of *The Apprentice* emailed me to ask for advice on the auditions; some even asked if I would meet them to give them a de-brief on the situation. But my advice was simply: be yourself. If you need someone to brief you on how to do that, *The Apprentice* is the wrong thing for you.

I worked my notice right up to the day before I went into the house. I was getting paid a day-rate before going into the house. My freelance contract was coming to an end, and because they had been very impressed with me they had offered me a permanent position. I did consider this, but decided to give *The Apprentice* a shot instead. After all, that's the sort of opportunity that doesn't come along very often. They said they were very sorry to see me go and definitely wanted me to get back in touch afterwards. Little did I know how different things were going to be when I walked out of that house as the winner.

CHAPTER EIGHTEEN

The Filming

When the day came, it was like being on an undercover operation. There was a car waiting outside with the windows all blacked out. I felt like I was on the A-Team! It was great. We pulled up at the location. My car parked on one side of the road, and I could see there were other similar cars dotted around. It was honestly like a secret mission and I was feeling, 'Wow, how exciting is this!'

I was also starting to feel absolutely shit-scared. I had no idea what I was letting myself in for. None. It didn't seem real.

I'd packed at the very last moment because I'd lost my police check forms and I wasn't sure I would be allowed on the show. I ended up not getting it back until midnight on the day before I was due to go on. I'd been out to buy a suitcase on the morning they were collecting me. My view was that there was no point packing if I wasn't sure I was going to get the suitcase in time and be allowed to go on, so I hadn't prepared anything, and it was too late by the time it arrived. I only started chucking a few things into my case the next morning just before they were due to collect me. I didn't care, really – I love last minute stuff like that.

All the black cars pulled into the location. A woman came over to the door of mine and started to explain what would happen next as she microphoned me up. The instructions came out like machine-gun fire.

'When you go through the door just walk and keep walking. You'll come to a reception area; go straight up to the desk and introduce yourself. There will be other people in the room, but never mind.

I took a huge breath. My heart was pumping and my hands were clenched as I walked through into the reception area, which was what you could see on the programme, all lit up in green. I didn't dare look anywhere except straight ahead at the receptionist. I managed to get out the words, 'Hello, I'm Michelle Dewberry, here for a meeting with Alan Sugar.' And then I had panicked thoughts about what to do next – should I step back, look around to see where to go? What happened next? Out of the corner of my eye I could see Jo, who I'd met at the interviews. She's the most excitable person I know and she was bouncing around trying to get my attention, mouthing, 'I knew you were going to come in! I knew it was going to be you!' I tried not to get distracted, so I stared straight ahead, but all I could see was Jo's hair in the corner, bouncing around.

One by one, the other contestants came in. No one spoke, everyone looked straight ahead. I was thinking how tough some of them looked and wondering how I was going to deal with it all. And then Syed entered. He literally *strutted* in. I just thought, 'Hmmm.' He was wearing a blue suit, blue shirt and brown leather shoes. Whereas everybody else had come in and stood still, Syed was wandering around to the water fountain, forward and back. I remember thinking, 'I'm not sure we're going to get on.'

There we all stood, in this room, lots of people, not knowing what on earth was going on, not allowed to speak. It felt like it went on for ever. I did feel reassured at seeing Jo. I liked her and we had swapped phone numbers at the auditions, but we hadn't contacted each other. Eventually we were sent through to another room, and I'll never forget the sight of Alan Sugar sitting on his chair with two people beside him – Nick and Margaret – at a huge table, studying us. We came in one at a time and he looked us up and down, seriously, never once smiling. There were cameramen in every corner, and of course as it was for a TV programme, I found it a bit weird. When we were in he said, 'Right …' and for those few moments I was so nervous.

He said, 'If you want a media career, you've come to the wrong place,' and I remember thinking that was a bit odd, as we were in a television programme, after all, but it was his call, he could say whatever he liked. When I played this bit of the show back, I saw that when he said, 'If you want to flutter your eyelashes around, don't bother – it won't wash with me,' they'd shown my face, looking really put out, which was odd because I wasn't put out at all – I certainly wasn't bothered about being told not to use any feminine charm on him!

We were driven back to 'the House'. We were going to live

on Millionaires' Row, the richest street in London. The house next door was for sale for millions of pounds. Lots of the others were really excited, but I remember feeling that they'd have to do more than that to impress me. We had to run in and explore our bedrooms, and everyone was exclaiming and saying 'Wow' like excited kiddies. In hindsight, we were so hyped up by the tension that we'd have cheered at anything. 'Wow – a bath!!! And a sink!!! And a toilet!!! Wow!!!'

It was very luxurious by normal standards and it had a fabulous pool in the back garden. There was a huge kitchen – very sociable – two lounges and masses of bedrooms. We had a champagne reception to celebrate our arrival and get to know each other, because it was the first time most of us had met. Everyone was talking over everyone else – either about themselves or about who was who among the other contestants. Once again I suggested we should go round one at a time in a round robin, to introduce ourselves and answer any questions, so we only had to do it once, rather than having to go over it all time and time again and shouting ourselves hoarse.

When it came to my turn I said I was in offshoring, and several of them wanted to know what that was. I was about to explain when Syed jumped in ahead of me and started to give his version of what he thought an offshore consultant was. I just looked at him and thought, 'Who is this guy?' because he'd got it all wrong. I was hacked off that he'd just taken over what I was saying. In my normal style, I just let him carry on speaking.

When he'd finished I said, 'Are you done? Do you want to say anything else about what I do for a living, or have you finished? Because everything you've just said is wrong. That's not what I do for a living at all. But I'm very impressed that you *think* you know what offshoring is.'

Jo chimed in with, 'Why are you telling us what she does for a living? Why don't you let her speak for herself?'

Quite a lot of people were tempted to be a bit bitchy in the first impressions they gave to the camera about their fellow contestants, but I wasn't. I would probably have said something mundane and boring about not really knowing anyone well enough yet, whereas a few of the others got quite stuck in about not liking the look of this person or that person. I sat and got quietly merry on champagne, thinking I couldn't be bothered bitching about anyone else. We had to choose a team name. Ruth had decided to make herself known at that point and ran the discussion, but, along with most of the girls, my attitude was, 'Does it really matter?' We came to a consensus in about ten minutes and got back to the champagne in the garden, but the boys took about three hours over theirs, which the girls found quite funny.

⌇

The next day we were driven over to Hackney, to the council estate where Sir Alan had grown up, for the first task. He asked us to say our team names and took us to the market, where we had to deal in fruit. Jo had been so excited. She was like one of those wind-up toys with white plastic feet on a spring that makes them go jumping all over the place. 'Wow!! We're going to sell fruit!! Wow!! We're going to get bananas, yaaay! And apples, yaay!!! And *sell*!' By contrast I was thinking, 'Fruit selling? Oh no, that means I have to get up extra early.' The rendezvous was 5 a.m. in Spitalfields Market. I was thinking, '5 a.m.? To buy fruit? Am I hearing things?' I wasn't as excited as I should have been, probably, but I'm one kind of person and Jo's another.

The girls had had a whole debate about what to wear to sell fruit. Some bright spark suggested that we should dress sexily and get the men to buy our wares because of how fit we were. Most of us were quite agreeable at first, the attitude being that if they were daft enough to pay for an apple just because we had our boobs out, that was up to them. We had a bit of a change of heart after that, though. I didn't have anything very sexy with me anyway, having tossed the clothes I'd brought with me into my bag in a hurry at the last moment. In fact not many of us had brought glammed-up things. Sharon was one who had. When she demonstrated her sexy look, the rest of us just sat and stared. Someone said, 'Woah, we can't go on the streets of Hackney selling fruit like that or we'll be arrested!' In the end we decided to dress in athletic clothes and go sporty. Despite this we still faced criticism for using sex to sell our wares.

We got to the market and split up into our teams. Karen was the project manager. I have to admit I took a bit of a dislike to Karen, because I felt she somehow thought she was above me. When we got to Spitalfields Market she lost our team mobile phone, which on that kind of task is a disaster as it was our only source of communications with the remainder of the team.

The rest of us went off on a recce to see what was what. I

With Sir Alan Sugar after winning *The Apprentice*, one of my proudest moments.
(Empics)

Main picture: The contestants line up with Sir Alan at the start of the second series of *The Apprentice*. I almost walked out as soon as I got to the auditions. (Fremantle Media)

Left: Ruth Badger and I had great fun posing for the cameras ahead of our final showdown. (Big Pictures)

Right: Syed and I grew close during the filming of *The Apprentice*. (Kent News & Pictures)

'What do I do with this?' In action during the Soccer Six charity tournament, wh[...]
my team made it to the final, only to lose to Brazil when I gave away a penalty.
(Empics)

Sitting on the *Big Brother* chair, with the lovely Esther Rantzen looking on, at the Childline Christmas Ball.

With Sarah Cawood at the *Closer* magazine Young Heroes ceremony, a really humbling occasion. (Getty Images)

At the after party for Ashlee Simpson joining the cast of *Chicago*. (Getty Images)

Left: Out in the West End with my friend Collette, November 2006. (Big Pictures)
Right: Taking a friend's son to the premiere of *The Snowman*, December 2006.
(Empics)

(Steve Double

remember saying to one of the wholesalers, 'Have you got any stuff we can have for free, please?'

He said, 'OK,' and gave me a box of bananas.

A little light bulb went off in my head. I was thinking, 'If I can get a box of bananas just by asking, what else can I get?' I knew that if we waited till market close we could get some pretty good stuff, as people would be desperate to get rid of it.

I went back to Karen and said, 'Why are we paying for this, why don't we just ask for it?'

She said, 'You can't do that,' but I said, 'Why not? They can only say no.'

We completely changed our strategy and I told the others not to buy anything, just to ask for it. We literally took over the market. It was full of girls darting around saying to the traders, 'What can I have for free?' We were given so much stuff. We got so much fruit that we had two vans full and had to leave some behind because we couldn't carry it. As a token of goodwill we thought we should spend some money, so we spent about £40. We got a bit above ourselves because the adrenaline was flowing, the energy was going and we were a big group of girls starting to have fun together. We gave a few kisses away and messed around. One guy we asked said, 'Yeah, take some bits,' and we got somewhat carried away. We got a forklift truck and just loaded it up. It was so funny. I remember us all leaning on this fork-lift, piled with free fruit, feeling very pleased with ourselves, when suddenly I was hit on the leg by a rat. I screamed, flipped, went absolutely ballistic. Then I heard everyone laughing. One of the stallholders had thought it would be hilarious to chuck his plastic rat at me. But it was the most lifelike thing I've ever seen and for a few moments I was terrified.

To me, asking for the free fruit was common sense. When you're negotiating, you start with your lowest possible value, which in this case was nothing, and work up from there. Why would you not give it a try? It's not insulting anyone, it's just asking. They say no, you say, OK, thanks, and you move on from there and find out their best price. I suppose I have a cheeky and probably quite naive attitude. Most people say they wouldn't dream of asking for something for nothing – I just thought it was a good idea.

Anyway, we sold our fruit at the market. We came up with all kinds of initiatives. We put it in baskets, making it look attractive, and altogether we were pretty gung-ho about the whole thing. It was great for me because I was doing things that I'd never done before – going up to people on the streets and selling fruit wasn't generally my line of work. I had one scary moment, when I got shut into a garage where some man made an indecent suggestion to me, but I declined politely and got out all right. Then I had a nasty encounter in Hackney with a dog. I'd gone into another garage not knowing there was a dog there until it started barking. It was a guard dog, in a cage at the end of a driveway, and it must have been asleep when I went past. Now it was awake and barking and there was no way I was going to be able to pass it going out. I went cold, became rooted to the spot. All my childhood fears came back. I lost the plot and started shaking and crying. The producer came over and asked what was wrong, and I explained I couldn't walk past the dog, even though it was in a big cage. In the end the producer had to hold my hand and lead me past, with my back squashed against the wall, petrified.

At the end of the morning we went back to the boardroom feeling incredibly pleased with ourselves, looking like the cats who'd got the cream. Sir Alan read out the profit made by the boys' team, and you could see they were thinking they'd done pretty well. Then he read out our results. When he announced we'd spent £40, you could see the boys' faces drop. Instantly their mood changed and they were trying to work out how we'd made such a small outlay. Then, when he announced our massive profit, Jo lost it. She was like Zebedee from *The Magic Roundabout* — I mean that in the nicest possible way. We were all high-fiveing and cheering. Even I felt genuinely excited. I was at least smiling, letting a bit of emotion out.

Then Sir Alan said, 'Hold on. I've got a real problem with you lot.'

His face was grim. We froze, hearing something in his tone of voice that was not going to be good for us. He proceeded to give us a massive dressing-down about the free fruit, telling us off for using our sex to our advantage, furious that one of the girls had massaged a trader's shoulders. They'd interviewed the trader with the fork-lift truck and he'd said, 'I don't know what happened, they railroaded me.' We were in a whole heap of trouble.

Sir Alan sent us out while he thought out our punishment; he was threatening to disqualify the whole team. We were appalled; we thought we were going to be thrown off the show. The boys were celebrating and telling us there was no way any of us were going to recover from this. I can't tell you how seriously we took it. It wasn't a game any more. We were in competition mode and we truly wanted to survive – to win.

When we went back in, Jo went mad. She was going, 'Don't you accuse me of using my sex to sell anything. I feel so strongly about this …' She was crying and banging the table and shouting at the boys and Sir Alan. It was awful. I was standing next to her, saying out of the corner of my mouth, 'Jo, this is not a good look. Calm down. Calm down.' Karen, the team leader, was trying to calm her down too.

Sir Alan said he'd had enough and wasn't going to be spoken to like that. He went out, then came back in and said we had five minutes to explain why we shouldn't be disqualified. Karen started to give him her reasons; Jo chimed in and started again. In the end he decided he would punish us by making us spend the same as the boys had. Even when he deducted their outlay from our profit, we'd won, so our team still came out on top.

It was a hollow victory; I felt like a naughty little schoolchild. I didn't want to go for the celebratory glass of champagne that had been arranged for the winners of the first task at Tower 42 champagne bar. When Jo heard, she was over the moon about it, but I was thinking, 'Oh, I go there on a Friday night after work.' To me it was just a bar near my office, a bit disappointing. The fact that we'd been severely told off had taken the gloss off our day and none of the rest of us wanted to go. It was awful. I didn't feel like going out and just wanted to go home, but the evening's event had all been arranged and we saw it through.

When I'd last seen Jo, straight after the judgement on that

round, she'd been crying hysterically, terribly upset by what had happened. Next time I saw her, outside Tower 42, she was bouncing up and down, back to her bubbly self, exclaiming how exciting it all was.

I said to her, 'Last time I saw you you were in tears. Now you're jumping up and down. You haven't even apologised for losing it in the boardroom, yet you expect us all to join in and have a good time. It's bizarre, I don't understand it.'

I didn't want to have a go at Jo – we're great friends now and I really like her. It's just that we're similar in some ways but so different in others that sometimes I find it really hard to understand her reactions to things.

We were a very subdued crowd that evening. We genuinely hadn't seen anything wrong in the way we'd carried out our task, so to be torn off a strip for it had really knocked us backwards.

CHAPTER NINETEEN
Communal Living

Generally, the atmosphere in the house was great. It was just like being part of a real family unit. We tried to have a rule that we left work at the door, so that we'd have time to relax. We used to cook for each other – we'd have great meals together and drink lots of wine and enjoy ourselves. I loved the dinner-table talk. We used to hang out together, get in DVDs and watch films. We were becoming friends. I was always the untidiest in the house by far, and I used to get into trouble with the other girls for it. I was always borrowing other people's things, sometimes without asking, because I thought it would be OK. I'd go and have a bath then wander downstairs wearing Jo's dressing-gown and slippers without asking, so I guess I was quite annoying to some of the other contestants, although hopefully in a nice way.

Our dressing-down over the fruit task had left its mark. When our team lost the next task, the ones not in the board-room were so relieved not to have been hauled over the coals that we fell into the house and decided to have a party to celebrate. We had a great time, dancing and singing, but also had far too much to drink. We drank everything we could find. We fell over, broke some glasses and were definitely way over the top; it was one of my best memories of the time there as the whole thing seemed so funny. When the boys came back from their treat for winning, they seemed drunk too. But the fact was that we got on really well as a group and had a lot of fun.

Naturally, in a group that size, personalities start to come into play and you find yourself more in tune with some people than others. We came from a wide range of backgrounds. I was completely Northern; Ruth was a popular character; Paul was hilarious at first, but he was good at creating what I call a spinning-top effect – pushing his hand up and down, making the top spin wildly, then stepping back to watch what happened. I started getting closer to Jo and Ruth, but I found I didn't particularly get on with Karen. You can't expect to gel with everyone in a situation like that. In the end, my mindset was, 'I'm here to get a job, not necessarily to make friends. I'm here to do my best and then go home.' I was happy to be myself and have a good experience, but ultimately we were all leaving at the end of it.

My initial impression of Syed hadn't been very favourable. At first I thought he came across as being arrogant, which I don't really like. But as time went on, things changed.

Unless you've experienced it, you can't understand the intensity of the experience of being in a TV show like that. We were together twenty-four hours a day, with very minimal contact with our friends and family outside. For me, it meant a lot of my support network was gone, as I'm a great one for ringing my mates and asking what they think of this or that decision or problem in my life. I like to bounce opinions off people and chat things through with people I trust – and suddenly that was all gone. Instead I was surrounded by strangers, not knowing who would stab others in the back to get ahead, or who was sincere. It takes me quite a while to get to know someone and like them, and it can take people time to get to know and like me. Sometimes people can misunderstand me and take a little time to recognise that my intentions are actually good.

Gradually, I began to see a different side to Syed. Yes, there was the confident, arrogant exterior that came over at first, but I was sure there was also a kind, caring person behind it. As the weeks progressed, the others would go to bed and Syed and I would stay up talking until two, three or four in the morning, even though we had to be up by six or seven. Despite being very different, we seemed to get along well. Every morning he'd make me porridge for my breakfast and hot water with lemon. The others in the house started winding him up about it, and he got shy, so he used to leave it in the kitchen where nobody would see. I thought it was the sweetest thing.

I really started to bond with him. I'd miss him if we were off on our tasks and I'd really look forward to getting home and seeing him again. At the outset it was more of an emotional attraction than a physical one, but there was a real connection between us. Nothing ever happened on a physical level while we were filming *The Apprentice*, but we did become close.

Team dynamics in *The Apprentice* has to be one of the most interesting factors for viewers – and with so many strong personalities competing to be noticed, it's not surprising that there were sometimes fireworks. In a normal work situation you're just part of the team with a shared goal to achieve. In a TV show, however genuine the tasks may be, things are still influenced by the fact that every one of the people taking part is under scrutiny for their performance. As usual, I tried to let this aspect of it all wash over me and just be myself, but there were always others looking for the opportunity to make a name for themselves. To anyone watching, I'm sure it's clear which personalities were determined to shine through.

Nevertheless, the tasks were a lot of fun. One of my favourites was the catering challenge. There was a festival and we had to organise an eatery that would make the most profit and get in the most customers. I loved it. Ruth and I had to go down to the Chinese supermarket to get ingredients, and we had such a laugh together, trying to give the impression that we knew what we were doing. I was learning by then that it was all about confidence – if you look like you're on top of the job, then people will have faith in you and you'll succeed far better than if you appear doubtful. Our team was selling noodles. Jo and I got dressed up as Chinese women and our job was to go round the local streets with samples, getting people to taste our wares. It was a lesson in how to sell – going out to the customer and showing them the product, convincing them to try it, so they would come to our stall rather than another food outlet. That's an important part about sales – don't wait for the customer to come to you.

It was hard graft. We didn't stop at all. I think that might be why I loved it so much – I really enjoy being busy and rushed off my feet, particularly if things are moving forwards. The whole day was really good fun, because I was doing stuff that I never thought I'd do in a million years. We were dressed in long satin dresses – mine was a size fourteen so I had to tie it in tight around my waist. I hadn't realised that I was going to be dressing up that day, and I hadn't bothered to shave my legs, so I was a bit concerned to find the dress was split up to the thigh. It was also really cold, but none of it mattered – it was great fun. We had such a laugh.

Despite my lack of inclination for retail, I liked the Top Shop task a lot too, although I did become somewhat notorious after that episode. The main reason I enjoyed it was because I was appointed manager, which is my favourite role and a position that I think makes full use of my own particular skills.

There were various posts that our team had to fill, with each of us fulfilling a particular role. Basically we had to sell more clothes than the other team.

My team for that task was Ruth, Sam and Ansell. Neither Sam nor Ansell could be the VIP stylist, because it was based in the women's changing room and you couldn't have a bloke hanging around in there all day, so that job had to go to either Ruth or me. I recognised that Ruth was likely to be a better saleswoman than me because that was her background, so the shop floor would be the best place to use her talents. The majority of the customers coming through would be there, so as team leader I decided that it would be silly to put my best salesperson in the VIP room away from the main flow of traffic.

Following that logic through, I had to be VIP stylist. The VIP suite wasn't a very active place to be as you were shut away from the main action, and of course I always like to be busy. The day before the task started I had to choose clothes for the rest of my team – part of my brief. I chose a stripy shirt for Sam and a T-shirt with what I was told was a 'cool' pink neck scarf for Ansell. The results were so funny. Sam looked like an escapee from the *Beano* comic, and Ansell looked like some sort of cowboy-cum-waiter with a table cloth around his neck. They were good sports, though, and both wore the outfits I had picked. But after that, it was a bit flat – I didn't have much to do. While I was in the room choosing the outfits and waiting for them to come back from the shop floor, I spotted a bottle of champagne in the corner. I asked if I could have a glass, because I was bored, and I was told I could. I had only had about two sips before someone came back in with some clothes and I put the glass down.

At lunchtime, the bad news came through that our sales were twenty-five per cent less than the other team, which meant we were well behind. It called for drastic action. As manager, I took a decision to change the structure of the team, as it wasn't working as effectively as it should have been. I recognised the VIP room wasn't working, so I put myself in the changing room on the shop floor and started using my stylist role to improve sales in the area with higher traffic. I'd say to customers, 'Oh, that's a nice pair of jeans, would you like to try a top to go with them?' and suggest something that might look nice. I also took the opportunity to converse with the other team's customers and cross-sell our products to them. Getting customers to spend money on our products was the key thing.

Our conversion rate of customers to sales then became huge. Not only did we catch the other team up, we also overtook them, despite having sent customers across to them by cross-selling. Syed was on the opposing team. However, we did help each other out. If someone came in for a winter coat and I didn't have any, I'd pass them to him, and if someone went to him for spangly dresses, he'd pass them to me. Our theory was that if they wanted a coat and there weren't any, they'd walk out, so we might as well help them find what they wanted. I might suggest something to go nicely under the coat, of course, but anything was better than losing a sale. We went from being twenty-five per cent down to five per cent up by late afternoon – a total improvement on our morning's performance of thirty per cent. It was amazing. I was really proud of the way we had turned that around. I think it might have been one of the reasons I stayed on the programme. Once again, I think I was able to take a cool look at what was going wrong, what the customer needed, and how we could provide it. Then I reallocated our team in the most effective way. Cool analysis and not being afraid to change an initial starting plan that's not working were what won the day.

The tasks we were set were quite sales-biased, but then being able to sell is an integral part of what Sir Alan Sugar's business is all about, so I think the show was good preparation for people going into his enterprise and what the winner would end up doing in the long term. The fact that I did so well pleases me particularly because I managed to compete with some of the best salespeople I've ever met – Ansell, Paul, Ruth and Syed, who did this every day. All the other finalists sold on a day-to-day basis too, and had done for years. Most of them had had professional sales training, but I hadn't. Apart from the odd stint as a shop girl in my teens, I'd never sold anything directly to the public or trade, certainly not as part of my career training.

I learned that selling isn't a case of, 'Do you want to buy this? How much? Right, thanks, bye.' You've got to make sure that you're targeting the right customer, develop a relationship and negotiate. You have to have good lines of communication with your suppliers, put good teamwork in place and get yourself a good deal. It's about marketing packages, adding incentives, luring people with a bargain. It was very interesting for me to learn all this, but I also felt my success was a testament to my adaptability. Considering I was competing against some of the country's top young sellers, I was proud of my performance. Members of the public might say, 'Oh yes, Michelle's not as good at some of the tasks as the others,' but then I never professed to be a saleswoman. I was a project manager. I could identify where a need was and put the best person into the role, but direct selling wasn't necessarily my forte. Management and strategy were.

My all-time favourite task was probably the cruise ship. I absolutely loved it – not because of the task itself, but because it stirred memories from my past. Being on the ship reminded me of Hi-de-Hi, which I used to watch when I was a young girl, and Butlins, where we went on family holidays. I felt like a redcoat. We put on a dancing competition, which I loved. We had to dress in daft uniforms, but everywhere we walked on the ship people would know us. We'd walk around, smiling, saying, 'Good morning, good morning,' until our jaws ached. We were on board to organise the entertainment for the passengers; to a budget, of course. I was disappointed to find I was on Paul and Ansell's team because Ruth and Syed were my friends and I'd have preferred to be with them, but it was still great. We joined the ship in Turkey and got off in Rome, stopping off at a few Greek islands.

I didn't get on as well with Paul and Ansell as I did with the other two, but we did have some laughs. I have a hilarious memory of Syed challenging Ansell to an arm-wrestling contest. Syed took it very seriously and was determined to win. He gave Ansell a real run for his money, but in the end he lost. It was one of those moments where I guess you have to be there to appreciate it, but it truly was a funny, funny moment.

At the end of the cruise we had a fabulous party. It was the first time we'd really had the opportunity to let our hair down, and because there was nowhere for us to go on board ship, we had it in one of the boat's nightclubs. Having not been partying anywhere for about six weeks, we were like kids in a candy shop. Syed was on the dance floor with some girls he'd met; I took to the DJ box, kicking out the resident DJ and MC-ing on the microphone, taking requests. Ruth was dancing; we were all pretty drunk. We didn't feel quite so clever the following morning. Every single one of us came out with a head that was banging and a hangover. It was the day of judgement, as well. Ruth and Syed ended up getting sent back to the UK, while I was sent to Rome with Paul and Ansell. I was really upset that out of my two closest friends, one of them would be going home. On the way to Rome we had to keep stopping on the way, so I could be sick. I get travel sickness too, which was not a good combination with the hangover. We had to keep stopping at dodgy Italian roadside loos – yuck!

For the final we were told we had to organise a party. The venue was Tower Bridge. Before the show I'd had an invite to a Bond party somewhere, so I decided I would do that. Then Sir Alan mentioned Bond as a possible theme in his introduction, and we very nearly cancelled it. But then we thought, Why cancel a very good idea just because of that? It was tried and tested, after all. There was no point in cancelling it out of pride.

I didn't really enjoy the final. It was a very emotional time for me. I had to pick my own team from the other contestants. I decided to pick the people best suited to the job, completely ignoring the previous conflict that had been evident among them. I shouldn't have ignored it because it ended up being a massive pain in the backside. Nobody seemed to like anyone else, and things kept going wrong. At one point, I forgot to file some paperwork, which meant we couldn't have lights or music during our event. I got a real dressing-down for that, of course.

The team spirit didn't improve as things went on. On the

actual night of the party, I ended up having an argument with Sharon. The moment I walked out of the lift she was right there, telling me the organisation was so terrible she was ashamed to be associated with it. I didn't appreciate that as we were just about to start the party. Unfortunately, the stress of a challenging and competitive task, combined with the strain of being constantly under the scrutiny of the cameras, does tend to make nerves and tempers fray. It's just another of the challenges you have to rise to.

I have to say, I don't enjoy events management. I'm about as creative as a peanut when it comes to that kind of thing. There's nothing hiding inside to be pulled out by the demands of a big party. That was why I hired Sharon – she was a good events manager. At the end of the day, you can't be good at everything, and a good businessperson recognises when they need to call in the experts. I know I'm not creative, and I'm not embarrassed to admit it. The trick is to focus on what you are good at and hire people to help you with the things that you can't do for yourself. There's nothing wrong with that at all.

But all the various arguments and petty disasters started to weigh on me. It was at that point that I found myself in the car, listening to the radio, waiting to go on the after-task treat that had been arranged for us. I felt really fed up. I was out of ideas. I'd had enough. Sir Alan had been on the phone having a go at me about the budget. The team weren't doing what they were hired to do. They weren't pulling together. I'd hired Syed for the team for my final – I'd been gutted when he was fired from the show – but unfortunately there was a lot of friction between him and Paul. If the two of them were anywhere near each other, I'd have to sit between them to stop them going for each other. The stresses were building up right across the team.

We had been filming the final on the anniversary of Fiona's death and I felt horrible. Then that song came on. Fiona's song. Without it I don't think I would have found the energy to go on, but I did. I knew she was urging me on in her own way, and that she was proud of me. At the end of the Bond party I was crying my eyes out. Ruth came over and gave me a hug and we both travelled back to the house together. I was completely exhausted. But I'd seen it through to the end.

Why did I emerge as the ultimate winner of *The Apprentice*? Plenty of people had their own ideas about it, and the battle between the Badger and the Blonde was certainly hyped up by the press, with articles in the business sections of papers that wouldn't normally acknowledge the existence of a reality TV show. The show was demanding and had real business lessons attached to it – there was far more to it than the cult of personality that rules something like *Big Brother*.

I think I came out on top for a number of reasons. Firstly, I did some great work on the tasks and Sir Alan recognised that. No one can say I'm afraid of hard work, and the combination of management talent and sheer graft certainly impressed him. There were some snide comments made about my background influencing the decision – but I think that distorts the picture. Yes, I had turned my early start into something good, but I didn't win because people made allowances for that. I won because of the strengths my self-made career path had given me. It was down to strength of character, rather than anyone feeling sorry for me.

I don't really regret anything I did on *The Apprentice*. I know I got some stick for drinking champagne when I was on the Top Shop task – but that's just my character – it doesn't mean I'm not worthy to win. I won because I have a strong ability. I might not articulate it in the way you might expect, the way the other contestants did. I don't agree with those who feel the need to pull everybody down to make them see my point of view. I think quite often if you tell everyone how great you are you end up hanging yourself. I prefer to just get on and solve the problems. I think Alan Sugar saw that all along.

My mum was a bit overwhelmed by it all. When she was interviewed after the final result was announced, she was asked, 'Did you always know that Michelle would win?'

She just looked at them in a bewildered way and said, 'No, no. I always thought it was going to be Ruth Badger.'

I nearly died. I was thinking, 'Mum you're not supposed to be saying that; that's not what you do.'

Without any shadow of a doubt, *The Apprentice* reinforced my belief that if you believe in yourself, you can honestly do anything. Anything at all. I feel that very strongly. I was nervous about some of the tasks, sure, but it was exciting, and we just had to crack on and do it, whatever doubts we might have privately. I look back on all that time I spent thinking the people in the house were better than me. They weren't. None of them. They liked the sound of their own voices and wanted to bang on about how good they were, but they were probably just covering up their insecurity. Humans are all the same. We all have a set of needs – to be loved, to be wanted and to grow. No one wants to be stagnant. People just respond differently in search of those goals. They might get loud or clever or sub-dued or exuberant to cover up their need, but we're all in search of the same things. Nobody's better than anyone else. What's different is that some people take steps to achieve their goals, and some don't.

How many people got the application form off the website and thought about filling it in? How many thought, 'They're never going to bother picking me, why should I bother?' Thousands actually sent it in, what about the rest who never took that first step? I don't have a magic wand to wave that just makes things happen for me. I know all there is to know about self-doubt. I could have left that hotel without even going for my audition, but in the end I saw it through. I might so easily have taken the easy way out and let the others talk over me, or given up – but I found the confidence to be myself. Believing in yourself isn't always easy. Sometimes you have to make that leap of faith and just give it the best shot you can. Niggling voices might pop into your head, but that's fine – you just need to be able to ignore them. Sometimes you need a bit of help from outside – you just have to be able to recognise it and act on it.

There was a moment early on in the filming when I was feeling a bit flat and depressed. I said to one of the team that I didn't think I was good enough to still be in it. She said to me,

'Look at it this way. Who, among the people who've been sent home, do you think is better than you? Which one should still be here instead of you?'

I said, 'None of them.'

'Well,' she said, 'if there's no one out of the people who have gone that you think should be replacing you, why don't you believe that you are good enough?'

That thought helped to turn me round. It kept me going through a lot of the bad times.

It's something that could apply to the whole process of interview and job selection we all have to go through. Yes, you may feel, when you walk into that interview, that you only have so many minutes to make a favourable impression – but don't be tempted to jump in with both feet. Plan ahead, assess the situation coolly, know what you want to say, and don't be afraid to listen before you speak. You need to sell yourself, but it has to be the real you that you're putting across – not someone that's gabbling out the first thing they think the interviewer wants to hear. Ask questions, if you need to, before you give answers. Make sure you understand what's being asked of you. Take time to play to your own strengths. You know what they are. Make sure you give yourself the chance to communicate them properly to your future employer.

Overall, taking part in *The Apprentice* was one of the most exciting and pleasurable experiences of my life. We got to do all these things that would never come our way in normal everyday life – producing a calendar with one of the top companies in the country, hosting a dance competition on a cruise ship, dressing up as a Chinese woman and shouting at people to come and buy noodles. It was amazing. Even now, every time I drive under Tower Bridge, I stop and think about the final and the moment I stepped out onto that stage to be announced as the winner.

The concept of *The Apprentice* is very inspirational to young people because it brings business to their fingertips. It makes work trendy and sexy and interesting. When I was at school I had no idea that London existed in terms of career options. If I had my time over again I'd like to be a trader in the City. I'd like to have been one of the best traders the City had ever seen – I'd have made it my life. Then I'd have retired early and taught people how to do the same. I suppose I could do it now, if I really wanted to – but I'm happy enough in the path I've taken.

A programme like *The Apprentice* does a lot to open youngsters' minds to the things they can potentially achieve, even if, like me, they don't come from a privileged background. People can be disparaging about reality TV and the contestants who sign up for it, but I think *The Apprentice* is in a class of its own. All fourteen candidates in that show were high achievers with an impressive list of past achievements. How many of our detractors can say that for themselves? My friend calls me a person of the common people. I'm just a normal person, with a normal life and normal ups and downs. I hope that the kids who watched *The Apprentice* look at me and think, hang on, she didn't do so well at school, she's from Hull, and she's made something of herself, I could try that too. My message to them is: if you don't fit into the conventional mould, don't beat yourself up. Understand why you're different, recognise what your strengths are, then concentrate on harnessing and developing them.

CHAPTER TWENTY

The Aftermath

After we had finished filming the show I took a few weeks off. I really needed to get away from everybody and everything. Much as I like to have family and friends around me, I need my own space, and living in a communal house under the surveillance of TV cameras with the added pressure of competition had been exhausting. It had been a weird, unreal time and I wanted to get my head straight before I started my new job. I flew to Egypt, alone, and had a wonderful time.

I had started working with Sir Alan in October 1995 when the filming finished. This was because there was a seven-month delay between us finishing filming and the winner of the show being announced. In May 1996, I was officially declared the winner of *The Apprentice* and was given a job with Viglen, one of Sir Alan Sugar's companies. My brief was to set up a company called Xenon Green, and the idea was that it would find a way of profitably recycling computers and electronic items, not only benefiting the environment, but also running as a viable business enterprise. I was determined to make sure that Xenon Green was a genuine business model first and foremost, so I set out to write a feasibility study. I had to make sure that the company would work before it was launched. This was not only essential in business terms, but I was also aware that if, six months down the line, it was found not to be viable, I would be publicly judged by the nation as a failure. No one would be interested in details – the headlines would put the blame squarely on the shoulders of *The Apprentice* winner.

I set about contacting all the businesses that worked in Xenon Green's field and investigating all angles of the market. I took some time to study the recycling market and to understand and evaluate how it worked. I also looked into the regulations surrounding the recycling of electronics, known as the WEEE and RoHS directives. I undertook financial analysis of the companies already in the market and looked at their performance. What were their profits? What were they turning over? What volume of waste were they dealing with to achieve those turnovers? I went on site visits in order to become familiar with all the different stages in the process, because I had to decide where Xenon Green should concentrate its efforts. It could be a collector, taking computers from offices and sending them to a recycler. It could deal with the process end to end – from collection through recycling to resale of the parts. Or it could just be a recycling company. I investigated logistics, outlay, risks, rates of return, customer profile, profitability time frames, future market trends, the lot.

Meanwhile, there had been developments in my personal life. As I've said, Syed and I had become very close during the time we'd spent on *The Apprentice*, although nothing physical had happened between us. After filming was over, we met up a couple of days later for coffee and it was just like it had been in the house.

As I have mentioned, there had been a gap between the end of filming and the transmission of the first episode of *The Apprentice*. As soon as the series hit the screens, we became well known. Suddenly, we couldn't go out together without attracting a great deal of attention. Before, we'd been able to go to restaurants, hold hands, do all the things normal couples do and nobody took any notice. But once people knew who we were, our lives turned around. If we'd been spotted together it would have been all over the papers, so whenever we did see each other, which was becoming increasingly rare because of my work commitments, we stayed in as we didn't want things to be public. All we ever did together was watch DVDs and get takeaways, which at first was great but ultimately put an increasing strain on our relationship. Being in the public eye also puts you under constant scrutiny and gives people a right to access your life. I found it difficult, but if you choose to put yourself on national television for twelve weeks, you can't resent the fact that people want that access. But trying to sort out our feelings with the worry about the eyes of the country being on us was very difficult.

Around the time the series first went out, I held what I called a launch party. One of the guests was the person who had first given me the application form for *The Apprentice*. He was a trainee journalist, but I'd felt it only fair to invite him as he'd started the whole process. After the party, a story appeared in the *Sun* about the relationship between Syed and me. I called him up and asked him if he had sold it to them. He categorically denied any connection with the story and told me he was terribly offended at my suggestion that he might compromise his integrity.

The next day I called him back. I said, 'I don't mean to be nasty, but are you sure it's not you? A few of my friends have been saying that there was a guy at the party who wasn't drinking but was wandering round asking an awful lot of questions.'

Again he swore that no way was it him.

A few days later he rang me back. He said, 'Michelle, I want to be honest with you. I've had a think and, yes, it was me that sold the story. I don't regret it and I'd do it again. At the end of the day I owe you nothing. I'm not your friend. I was never your friend, yet you told me everything.'

I told him I thought what he'd done was disgusting and very wrong. I felt that I'd treated him as my friend and he'd let me down. Maybe I'd trusted him too easily, but he'd betrayed that trust. His response was that it was my own stupid fault for inviting him to the party knowing he was a journalist.

I said, 'Well, you've been very silly. I'm going to get better known as the series progresses and I'm sure I could have helped you. You could have come to me as a friend and asked me to do something with you as you were trying to get into journalism. I would have helped you. One day, I'm sure you'll regret what you did.'

A few days later he rang me and said he was sorry and did regret what he'd done. He said he felt very bad about it and asked me to forgive him. I wished him well with his career but made it clear I didn't want to speak to him again. How did I know what his motives were for calling me? Any trust that might have existed between us was gone.

That experience was just a small taste of what was to come.

My background had been hinted at in the TV show, though not by me, and obviously people had a natural curiosity to find out more about it. I suppose it was to be expected. My past, like anyone's, is relevant to who I am today, so it is a necessary part of my story. There was a lot of speculation, and people who were or had been close to me decided to seize the opportunity to start selling stories about me. That really, really hurt. People thought they had the right, without even asking me, to sell pictures of me, letters I had written and stories about me. It was a valuable lesson in being careful who to trust, but I learned it the hard way. I normally tell everyone everything and now realised how foolish I had been.

Around the time that the final was on air, the speculation about me was rife. Lots of people were selling stories and most of the newspapers and magazines were trying to get me to sell my side of the story. Originally I was very against this as I wanted to keep my private life exactly that. But one day, almost as soon as I had won, one of the Sunday newspapers called me and told me that my uncle had sold his story exposing everything about my family life. As this was an uncle I did not get on with – he was my dad's brother – I was worried about what he was going to write. I decided to re-evaluate my decision not to give an interview. I spoke to my family and asked if they would be happy for me to disclose personal details. They were. I spoke to one of the newspapers and decided that since my life was going to become public knowledge that weekend, I was going to have my say. I saw it as an opportunity to set the record straight. It was also an opportunity to earn some money to pay for the medical treatment of a very close family member who was ill.

I signed a deal with a national newspaper. As soon as I'd agreed to give the interview, I began to have second thoughts. I didn't sleep a wink the night before. In the morning, I was pacing up and down, ringing my close friends and family and my then agent, asking whether I should go through with it. I had a sick feeling in my tummy. The nerves got so bad I ended up throwing up in the kitchen sink.

The paper had sent a car for me and it was sitting outside the door, but I couldn't bring myself to go out – it felt all wrong. There were about ten people waiting for me in a hotel in central London – reporters, photographers and so on – but I couldn't face them. They kept ringing me to say, 'Why aren't you here? You're late.' After about an hour I decided it was a necessary evil, because I wanted to raise the money for the medical fund. On top of which, I knew my uncle's story was coming out and I needed to combat the rumours flying round about me. But it still didn't feel right.

I should have trusted my instincts. They recognised, of course, that the part of my story that would sell papers was the bit about how violent my dad was. Everything that was said was true, but it wasn't the whole story. They put a lot in about how he'd forced my sister to leave home and how at one point I'd even wondered if he'd been responsible for her death. When the paper came out and I saw the headline MY KILLER DAD, my reaction was, *Oh, shit. He hasn't killed anyone. He's not a killer.* I just thought, 'Michelle, what have you done?' Seeing episodes from my life laid out in cold print was a real shock. I was worried that people would see me as selling out, exploiting my background with no thought for how my family would feel, when the opposite was true. My only consolation was that, by donating one hundred per cent of the payment for the article, I knew I had helped provide medical care for someone who really needed it.

One of the reasons for writing this book is to set the record straight once and for all. I don't see myself as a victim, but stories like that which present only the bad parts of my past want to make me look like one. They didn't lie – what they reported was fact; but they didn't show the positive things that came out of my past.

If I didn't actually agree to give them an interview, it seemed that papers were happy enough to fill in the gaps themselves as they pleased. A picture of me looking like a bitch appeared on the front page of one national newspaper, with a headline saying: 'Fat, cocky, lazy, loud, grumpy, bitchy – what *The Apprentice* winner really thinks of her fellow contestants – and her boss.' It had me calling Alan Sugar 'Mr Grumpy', Karen 'Ice Queen Bitch', and the others all sorts of things. It was awful. I've no idea where they got it from. They had people saying I'd called them a 'slap-head', which is truly not the kind of word I'd use about someone else. All I can think is that they'd picked odds and ends from the show, such as me saying 'I really don't like Karen', or calling Paul an idiot during an argument, and stuck them all together, making them look like a string of insults. They had me calling Jo a 'crazy red-head', which really upset me because she's one of my very good friends. They made it look like I'd told them all these things, but the only time I spoke to that particular paper was when Ruth was in the room with me, before I'd even won – and I certainly hadn't said anything like that then. Another newspaper then went to Karen and said, 'Look at this, Karen, Michelle says she really hates you. What have you got to say about Michelle?' So Karen was goaded into doing a whole interview saying how she hated Michelle, and Michelle had only won because she had blonde hair. The whole thing was nonsense.

As my feasibility study progressed at work, my instincts and research began to tell me that Xenon Green was not likely to fulfil its brief of short- to mid-term profitability with low outlay. However, I wanted to give the project a fair chance and continued to look at it in a non-biased way. As time went on and I learned more, I became more and more certain that the company was not going to achieve the objectives that Alan Sugar wanted it to. I asked for a meeting with him, presented my report and explained that I didn't think it was a feasible market for him to enter for an early profit. I laid out all the options before him and he went away to think what he wanted to do. After Sir Alan had read my feasibility report, he came back to me saying that he accepted my assessment that the company was non-viable. He then asked me to embark on another project for Amstrad, upgrading internal CRM

(Customer Relationship Management) systems.

While I had learned a lot in the time that I had spent with Sir Alan both before and after winning the show, I was really disappointed that Xenon Green had not worked out. I had worked so hard to win the job and had given up an exciting and lucrative City career to be a part of Sir Alan's empire. I had really high hopes of being the driving force behind an exciting and innovative new company which, at the outset, we believed had the potential to be a valuable asset to his portfolio. Unfortunately this was not the case and once the decision had been made not to progress with Xenon Green, I naturally started to ask questions about what my future held in the organisation. After speaking with Sir Alan, it became apparent that there were no similar opportunities to develop a new enterprise within his organisation and the remainder of my contract would be filled with internal projects. While I totally understood the rationale for this, I couldn't help but feel disappointed and I started to think about the life I'd left behind. The main reason I'd come to London was to develop my career and experience the buzz of the city lifestyle. My office was located outside St Albans, and with no Xenon Green or similar position, I couldn't see how my career was going to develop. I decided to rethink.

CHAPTER TWENTY-ONE

My Baby

Although I had now moved on from the Xenon Green project, things were about to get more complicated when I discovered that I was pregnant. Syed, of course, was the father. Because of my endometriosis, I'd always believed that I couldn't have children, so it came right out of the blue. One day I had incredible tooth pain which was so bad that I ended up driving to the A&E department of a local hospital. It turned out to be an abscess. While I was there, I also mentioned that I had been suffering from bad tummy pains. They examined me and told me I was expecting a baby. I was in total shock. In some ways I was overwhelmed by the miracle of being pregnant when I didn't think it was possible. In other ways, it felt as though my world was crashing down. I'd just won *The Apprentice* and found myself being held up as an icon to many people. I had received literally thousands of emails from people saying they admired me, supported me and wanted to be like me, who held me up as a role model. Now I was so confused. I felt I'd let everyone down and did not have a clue what to do next.

I had the most horrendous morning sickness. I was very ill. I remember throwing up all day at work, getting in the car to go home and having to stop about six times on the way. The last time I couldn't stop and was sick over myself as I drove. It was horrible; I had a really bad time. My hormones were all over the place, I felt low and had severe pains right from the beginning. The stress just built and built. I felt so overwhelmed and needed to talk to somebody. I told my friends that I was pregnant so I could hopefully have their support, but quickly realised it was a foolish mistake as one of them promptly sold the story to a tabloid newspaper, which increased the pressure tenfold. I still don't know who it was, but it absolutely destroyed me. I was only just pregnant, hadn't come to terms with it and hadn't even passed the safety zone, and now the whole nation knew I was pregnant and was judging me. I was devastated.

Syed then had to tell his family, who are practising Muslims and had no idea that he'd even been having a relationship with me, so news that I was expecting came as a real shock. Both Syed and I are responsible people, and both of us wanted to do the right thing. We had so many options available to us and all the options had so many different positives and negatives. It was just an overwhelming, all-consuming blur. If we wanted to make a go of things, there was an element of pressure on me to convert to Islam. For the sake of my baby and to consider all the options, I gave it some very serious thought and read up on it. There's a lot about Islam that attracts me – it can be a very peaceful, calm religion, and, sadly, in the West at the moment, quite misunderstood. The teachings make a lot of sense and I respect them.

The shock hit both Syed and me hard, and unfortunately there was an intense amount of press interest in our news. They camped outside the house. People were selling all sorts of stories – half-truths and downright lies. I was followed in the street, and tailed while driving my car. I felt threatened. I took to phoning friends and giving them a description of the person following me – just in case. Once I was convinced that someone was about to push me onto the tube track, in front of a train. In the end I became reluctant to go out and felt like a prisoner in my own house. I even had the doorbell removed to stop reporters ringing it. I was so consumed in this bubble that I felt my life seemed to be falling apart. There were all these rumours flying round about me, including one that Sir Alan was furious about the baby and had put me on gardening leave. That simply wasn't true. But there was no getting away from the fact that I was public property. One man came up to me in the street and demanded, 'Why aren't you at work? You've been sacked!' I asked him what business he thought it was of his, but he replied, 'I think you'll find, young lady, that it's the nation's business.'

I had to concede privately that he was right.

Syed and I were so miserable and confused that another option we felt we had to consider was terminating the pregnancy. A part of me didn't want to: what if this was the only chance I had of being pregnant? But I was so unhappy that I took the step of booking an appointment at the clinic. At the same time, I grew to really love my baby. It felt so good knowing that I had a child inside me – I had always wanted a family of my own.

I was terrified. I cancelled the appointment, then rang up and booked another. Even though I loved the baby so much, I kept booking myself in for a termination because I was so confused. The hospital staff were very kind, and never complained that I hadn't turned up to the appointments. Week after week I booked myself in, and week after week I couldn't bring myself to go. I think it was like a safety net, just having the appointment. I didn't want to end the pregnancy, but I couldn't see my way ahead.

Syed and I were desperately trying to work out what was for the best. After much deliberation, he suggested that we should get married, with the expectation that I became a Muslim at some point in the future. It all seemed so overwhelming. I want nothing more than to be married with children and I really cared about Syed. But we had previously encountered commitment problems, and I just couldn't see beyond them. I could have stayed as I was and become a single mum, but I began to panic. What if the child, when it was older, chose its daddy's religion and I didn't? Would it think my way of life was wrong and reject me? Or, even if it didn't, would we be separated after death? Deep down, I wanted my baby more than anything, but I wanted it as part of a happy, united family. It was an unbelievably difficult and confusing time.

One morning, I had a hospital appointment and was just feeling beside myself with confusion. I had no idea which way to turn or what to do. When I got there I asked to see a professional counsellor for the first time to discuss my feelings. While I was there the pains in my tummy became agonising, and I started to lose blood. I was kept in, and later that day ended up losing my baby.

I was absolutely devastated. I felt such a sense of loss, that my little one was gone. They had told me once that I was unlikely to conceive because of the endometriosis, but I had. What if my only chance of having a family was now gone? It was a terrible, terrible time.

I had to stay in hospital. Syed looked after me and was really good. After everything I had been through, I felt so pleased to see him but we were both truly devastated. We decided to announce what had happened to the press in the hope that we would be given some privacy, and they respected our need for space and let us be. I don't know how I would have coped if the papers had carried on trying to get pictures and interviews.

As it was, when I went home I went into a state of virtual collapse. I was seriously depressed. Friends tried to encourage me to get up and go out, but I couldn't. I felt that I couldn't face people looking at me and judging everything I did. I cut off my contact with friends and family. I wouldn't get up, wouldn't shower, wouldn't even answer the phone. I didn't respond to emails or texts or calls or knocks on the door.

Once again, I felt like I had lost control and was heading towards rock bottom at 100 miles per hour.

CHAPTER TWENTY-TWO

Recovery

In bleak times like those, it's your family and friends you turn to. I'd tried to cut myself off from everyone, but thankfully some of my mates refused to take no for an answer. One day, when I was having a particularly bad day, I rang my friend Vicky, who was in Hull. She desperately wanted to come round and see me, but she was too far away, and anyway I felt too low to want company. But Vicky didn't give up there. She rang Syed, who tried to call me himself, but I refused to pick up the phone when I saw it was him, knowing that he was only calling me because Vicky had told him to. In the end my friend Leigh rang, and because I didn't realise Vicky had her number, I answered the phone, imagining I could fool Leigh into thinking I was OK. I was very depressed and just wanted to be left alone, but Leigh insisted on coming round to be with me. Leigh and Vicky have been good friends to me. They put up with me discussing my problems over and over again, even though I never take their advice until I'm absolutely sure of it in my own mind. They're my closest friends.

My hormones were playing havoc with me as my body was still reacting to the end of the pregnancy and I was grieving for my lost baby. The support of my female friends was great, but ultimately I knew that the decision about how I was going to pull myself through was down to me and my own mind-set. As usual, I knew that my life was my own responsibility and that I was the one who had to find the strength to do something with it. But you can only sort yourself out when you want to – you have to be ready to take the first step for yourself.

My mum was on holiday at the time, so I couldn't turn to her for help. In the end I telephoned a very close family friend, called Moira, who was amazing. She's a near neighbour of my mum's, and our two families are very close. Her two boys are the same age as my two youngest brothers, and I've known them all since I was sixteen. Moira's reaction was firm.

'Come home. Come back to Hull,' she said. 'Come home. We'll look after you.'

So I went.

It proved to be the turning point for me. I was suddenly back to normality. There was no press, no pressure, no religious quandary, no on-off boyfriend. It was as I had been pre-*Apprentice*. Moira put on a Mexican dinner party. We danced, drank Tequila and had a great, uncomplicated good time. I laughed so much. I realised that I hadn't laughed like that for months.

I think I had basically become trapped in a post-*Apprentice* bubble, cut off from the real world. I was constantly worrying about what people thought about me, and constantly upset by all the negative things that had been written about me in the papers. I made the mistake of reading them all and storing them up inside, even though I knew they weren't true. It's easy to do. It really isn't nice, reading about yourself. Here were people who didn't know me, telling the nation who I was and what I was and discussing my pregnancy and my job as if they knew everything about me. I had chosen to remain silent and allow people to say what they liked about me without getting drawn in to mud-slinging in the press myself. I wanted to maintain my dignity. But Syed dealt with things in a different way. He wanted to put his side of the story across and felt that if others were talking about him, he was perfectly entitled to set the record straight.

Syed and I have been through some really intense times together, and because I carried his child he's always going to be someone who's special to me. We'll have lasting memories. Ultimately, though, I recognised that he was not the right partner for me, and trying to maintain a relationship with him was going to be destructive. Circumstances had brought us together and circumstances forced us apart. Going back to Hull for a few days helped me burst out of the bubble I had been living in. I found that what people wanted to talk about was me – Michelle – and whether I was all right and how I was feeling. Not Michelle, the Apprentice, and what the latest gossip about me was. Feeling that people cared about me as a person helped ground me. There were no appearances to keep up. I didn't have to do anything or be anyone except myself. It's a terrible strain when you can't go on the tube or buy a pint of milk without people wanting to photograph you or tell you what they think of you. Hull was just home. There was time for reflection.

Everyone has setbacks; no one can be unaffected by the things that happen to them. It's the nature of life. You need time to get over them. Losing a baby is a huge thing – and losing it in the public eye made it big beyond all proportion. Retreating to Hull helped me regain my perspective on life. I'd lost the baby, and however much I wanted to change that, it wasn't going to happen. I had to accept it as something that wasn't meant to be and move on, rather than letting it destroy me.

I've always been quite spiritual, and on the way back to London I went to see a fortune-teller – a serious medium that my family knows. I hadn't been to her before, but the visit really helped me. She filled me with a lot of positive thoughts and gave me the reassurance I needed. Obviously she knew a lot of stuff about me from the papers, but she saw beyond that. She said she knew I was worried that I'd never have children again, but reassured me that I would. It was as if a big weight had been lifted off me. She also told me that my baby's being looked after by Fiona. That gave me great comfort. I do believe there's an afterlife and that I'll be reunited with the people I love, and I was happy to think of them together.

When I got back to London, the support and love I'd received in Hull continued to buoy me up. My sister's boyfriend made sure he sent me an uplifting text message every day, so when I came back home there would be messages like: *Stay positive. You've always been my inspiration. Keep your strength. Get back to being a leader, because I want to follow you.*

Their acceptance of me helped me get back on track and regain some of the confidence I'd lost. It wasn't all straightforward – I collapsed with a painful haemorrhage and had to be admitted to hospital again. But I didn't let it get me down. I was once again on the road to recovery.

⁂

By the time I returned to London I'd made some decisions about my future. Once more, I started to re-evaluate my goals and decide what to do workwise. Sir Alan told me he was pleased with my work and said I could continue working on the internal projects.

I admitted that I had joined Amstrad to be mentored and develop my career and while I recognised that it was the right decision not to progress with Xenon Green, I still felt that launching and developing a company was the next stage in my career. If that wasn't possible within Amstrad, I wanted to set up a company of my own. I recognised that I missed working for myself and started to think back to my original goal of running my own consultancy. My heart was back in both consultancy and the City. After almost a year of working for him, I decided to take the brave step of leaving the security of Sir Alan, taking with me all the knowledge that I'd learned from him, and branching out on my own again. All my friends thought I was silly to walk away from a six-figure salary, but I explained to them that I was confident in my abilities to be self-employed and that life isn't always about living within the comfort zone. I believe that if something is not working, you have to make the decision that is right for you. The only difference with me was that I had the whole nation watching and passing judgement. However, I certainly wasn't going to let that stop me achieving my goals.

I respect Sir Alan tremendously and I learned a lot from him. One of the biggest things was to listen to other people, take on board the views they expressed based on their own understanding and standpoint, but ultimately make your own decisions. If you believe in something, even if those around you don't share that belief, you have to have faith in your own abilities. You have to be like a dog with a bone. One of the things I most admire about Sir Alan is that he's very confident of what he wants to be and where he wants to be heading. He also knows what he doesn't want. I think he respects those qualities in me too. When I left he wished me well and said that if he ever had a similar project to Xenon Green to evaluate, he wouldn't hesitate in using my business to do it. He understood and respected my decision and wished me well. There was a lot of nonsense written in the papers about how I came to part company with him, but ultimately it was a career choice like any other. I left Amstrad on good terms. I feel that if I had a business matter that I needed guidance on, I could approach Sir Alan and ask for his assistance. I have a great deal of respect for his acumen.

On a personal level, I did something I'd been considering for a good few months before *The Apprentice* and went on a three-day self-development seminar run by Anthony Robbins. It took place in one of the London exhibition centres – and there were ten thousand people there. I'd never been in a room with that many people before and as I looked round I thought, 'More people than this applied for *The Apprentice*, yet it was me that won!' So that was a positive start. The seminar taught us about overcoming limiting beliefs about ourselves, and helped me put the temporary phase of depression I'd been in after the loss of my baby into perspective. It made me see how many opportunities and good things in life lay ahead of me.

On the first night we had to do a fire walk. I had to walk, literally, over burning coals. We had to get ourselves into a state where we were investing our minds with positive energy. Ten thousand of us were in the pitch-black, in the pouring rain, with no shoes and socks on, chanting, 'Yes, yes, yes' to the beat of African drums.

The coals were supposed to represent something we wanted to overcome – a barrier we wanted to smash through that was holding us back from happiness. For me, the coals were the media pressure, the grief of losing the baby and all the negative parts of my experience. I had to visualise how I would feel getting to the other side and leaving them behind.

I walked in the line towards the coals, chanting, 'Yes! Yes!' I looked at them and they were really burning hot. I kept chanting, 'Yes!' Then I got to the front, and it was my turn. I chanted, 'Yes! . . . Fuck! No!' and ran away from them. But the guy in charge shouted to me to get back and face them.

'No chance,' I said. 'They're burning. There is no way in this land I'm walking across them.'

He pulled me back. 'What's your name?'

'Michelle.'

'Michelle, why are you running away from these coals? What are these coals?'

I told him.

He said: 'Face those fears!'

And I did. I walked across the coals. I ended up with a few blisters on my feet, but it was worth it.

The seminar taught us to visualise what we want to be and put aside the things we fear which hold us back. We had to affirm our strengths in order to help us live up to our potential. Here's what I put about myself:

> *Be: an aspirational, confident woman.*
> *Acknowledge: that you are a role model.*
> *Balance: business and pleasure.*
> *Show: you are a multi-faceted woman.*
> *Believe: in yourself!!!*
> *Live: this moment! Make it your own!*

That course was another turning point for me. Finally I was able to put the past behind me and begin to move on to the next phase of my life.

CHAPTER TWENTY-THREE

Anything is Possible

I set up my own company, called Michelle Dewberry Ltd. After leaving Amstrad, I threw myself into the dual task of developing this enterprise alongside the media opportunities that had arisen out of my appearance on *The Apprentice*. MD Limited, as it's known, offers consultancy services in all the major areas of expertise I've developed. I plan soon to extend it into a consortium of businesses, specialising in consultancy, training and property. I have already begun assessing the feasibility of the training company.

Currently, MD Ltd offers a variety of business services, especially focusing on offshore/outsource advice and guidance, as well as due diligence, project and programme management and business marketing advice.

I'm also realising my dream of mentoring people whose careers have become stuck in a rut; or those whose education didn't follow the conventional path and who would like to maximise their abilities in the workplace. I really want to mentor young people and help them turn their lives around. I want to explore media campaigns that will reach out and help kids who are finding that the conventional school route to employment doesn't suit them. There are opportunities out there, and even if you don't do so well at school, you can succeed. I hate the thought that there are still children destined to fail because of their background. There can be a sort of hereditary acceptance of failure or non-achievement, which I want to use my time in the public eye to fight. I want to break down the assumption people have in some areas that they leave school and go straight onto the dole. There is too much of a yob culture around, and kids have trouble seeing beyond the limitations of their social boundaries. If you look around you and say, 'This is where my family comes from – I'm proud of them, but I want to do more and be the best I can be,' then you can move on to fulfil your own potential, not mould yourself to fit someone else's.

I'm frequently asked to give lectures on business topics and I'm always delighted to have the chance to visit schools and talk to their students about my career path and the choices I have made. I would like to think that I open the students' minds to the opportunities that exist for them and motivate them to achieve their goals. I want people to look at me and say, 'If she can do it, everyone can.' I get a kick out of success, but I get more joy out of helping others succeed, particularly when the odds are stacked against them.

Today, one of the most important things in my life is to ensure that other families suffering from domestic violence are not left without a lifeline. My childhood experiences have made me determined to do what I can to protect women and children in similar situations. When my appearance on *The Apprentice* turned me into a household name, I realised that I could use my high profile to do something positive, and so I became closely involved with the organisation Women's Aid. Some of the background work I've done for them has been away from the cameras – visiting refuges is a private and personal experience that I have no wish to turn into a media event. However, I have agreed to become the face of a Women's Aid campaign, and I hope that the account of my childhood in this book will help people understand just how much that means to me.

I'm currently involved in their campaign to promote awareness of this issue among employers. Many businesses fail to recognise that some of their staff may be victims of domestic violence. We want to show them how to spot it and what they can do to help. People often see domestic violence as something embarrassing, and the victims will wrongly blame themselves. People sometimes feel that the workplace is for work alone and that personal problems should be left at home; this can make people feel uncomfortable about coming forward to admit what's happening. The workplace is where you spend a large part of your day and it's generally a safe place away from what's happening at home. It should offer an ideal opportunity for victims to take the first step in seeking help.

A very different opportunity for charity work came up when I was invited to appear on BBC's *Celebrity Scissorhands* as part of the Children in Need appeal. A team of well-known people was asked to train in hairdressing and beauty treatments in order to staff a salon offering pampering to stars appearing on Children in Need night. It was no light undertaking – we had three weeks' training to complete and were all offering our services completely free of charge – but I agreed. It appealed to me because it was an opportunity to do a great deal for a charity that is very close to my heart; and it was an opportunity to learn a very cool skill. It's always going to be handy to know how to cut hair. It turned out to be good fun.

I got on really well with all the other celebrity trainees and made some good friends. Steve Strange, from the eighties pop group Visage, was one of the show's great characters. He's such a gentle, sweet man, and was game for anything, but occasionally he'd wind me up because he'd do anything to avoid folding up towels. It was really hard graft, starting at eight in the morning and finishing at eight at night. There was one half-hour break during the day. It was a real eye-opener for me, having been used to working in an office, sitting at a desk and getting a cup of tea brought whenever I want one. In a hairdresser's you're on your feet all the time. We had to wear high heels as we were supposed to look smart for the customers, so our feet were in agony. You can't just slip away to the loo whenever you want to, you have to wait until you haven't got a client. You can't get a drink unless you're officially on a break. It's bloody hard work, and you have to be really nice at all times to everyone who comes in – even if they're rude to you.

One customer came in, and I was giving him a really good haircut. I was being mentored by Ben, who's Posh and Becks' hairdresser. He was getting a really cool do. As he came in he was telling me he was pleased to have an appointment with me as he didn't want any of the boys, especially Steve, cutting his hair. We were chatting as I did his hair, and I asked him if the salon was what he'd expected it to be. He said, 'Yeah, it's just a bunch of Z-list celebrities cutting hair.'

Emma Samms, the actress who was in *Dynasty*, wasn't happy to hear him say that, as we'd all given our time for free and she thought it wasn't right for him to sit and insult us. She refused to make him a cup of tea because he'd been rude. Darren Day, who's in a lot of West End musicals, heard about it and called me into the training room, saying we should do something about this guy. We got really mischievous. Darren went in to tell him that I'd been called away on urgent business and that he was getting Steve to finish the haircut. The guy almost broke down in tears because he didn't want Steve touching his hair. At the end Steve made him apologise for being rude to us. But we thought it was funny.

We formed a good team. Everyone was lovely. I preferred being a manager to a trainee, surprise, surprise. When it was my turn as manager, I ran a really tight ship, but I think the producers wanted to throw a lot of problems at me to see if I could cope. I was five staff members down out of our nine celebrities. Our three experts were called out of the salon in the middle of what they were doing, without warning, and I was left to manage without anyone supervising. The remaining four of us had clients, plus those that had booked in for the five other trainees who weren't there – plus the professional hairstylists' clients. On top of that they told us we had to cancel any beauty treatments that were booked in, telling us we weren't allowed to do them unsupervised. I'm sure it was a test – but I ended up doing really well.

I was delighted when I was voted through to the final night as a stylist, on the public vote. It was a real confidence booster – it meant the public had really liked me in some way, shape or form. The night itself was good fun. We met some great people, including Aggie from *How Clean Is Your House?*, who's become a good friend of mine. Another highlight was putting fake tan all over the lads from *Two Pints of Lager* who were going on to do a 'Club Tropicana' number. Will Mellor was really cute! They were hilarious. Ralph Little went into the changing room to put on the paper underwear for the tanning and kept saying, 'I can't come out because all my bits are showing.' I just told him to get out, it was nothing I hadn't seen before – but when he emerged, you could see everything. I had to send him back to put on a second pair of paper pants to make it less see-through and maintain his modesty. I got them all to do a sample of their Wham song in the dressing room. The whole night just flew by.

I've done quite a bit of TV work since *The Apprentice*. *Something for the Weekend* was great fun. I spent the morning with them, did an interview and then helped them cook and tasted cocktails.

I've also had a lot of fun taking part in publicity shoots for magazines. Depending on the subject matter, it can be an amazing thing to do. How many people in life get the opportunity to appear in one of the country's biggest magazines, with a team of experts making sure you look glamorous, taking you to some fun location to be the centre of attention? It's like a treat – a 'pinch yourself' moment – because it isn't something that comes your way in the normal run of business life. My favourite shoot was when the *News of the World* wanted to take photos of me rally driving and introduced me to David Coulthard. That was great. We even had the chance to go to an after-grand prix party with all the drivers.

Hello! did a really nice shoot with me as well. You get your hair and make-up done and have to pose in different clothes in glamorous settings. Their dressers bring clothes and I choose which ones I'm prepared to wear – I know my own mind! Some of the stylists have encouraged me to wear brighter colours; normally I wear a lot of black, but they've got me thinking that colours can suit me too. It annoys me when people say that I can't be a serious businesswoman and do this kind of thing. Why not? It's my spare time – it's irrelevant to work. It's a bit of fun and I do feel quite privileged to be in those situations. What's wrong with making the most of them? My attitude is that I'll do these things as long as they're either fun, teaching me a new skill or benefiting a charity. For example, I'd love to do *Strictly Come Dancing*. It's got nothing to do with business, but I love dancing, so why not?

So where do I go from here? Well, I look at this as the beginning of a whole new exciting chapter in my life. I'll be building up my business, mentoring other people, giving business talks and doing a whole load of things for charities close to my heart. I'd like to do some more travelling too. I'd love to go to

Australia, New Zealand, Thailand. Ultimately what I want from life is probably the same as most people – to be loved, happy and part of a family. I have my spiritual side, which is just as important to me as my driven, materialistic ambitions. My family in Hull is all-important to me, as are the friends who've supported me through the difficult times in my life.

One of my resolutions is to spend more time doing activities I enjoy for their own sake. I love looking at paintings and exhibitions, and I'm planning to try my hand at some artwork for my living room. I already have two blank canvases standing by, waiting for me to start painting. Exploring the business opportunities that have arisen out of the high profile I achieved when I won *The Apprentice* has taken up a lot of my time recently, but I'm determined to make sure there's plenty of time and space in my life for me to carry on growing as a person. I try to resist the temptation of working all hours just to prove a point – to listen to my own advice of working 'smarter, not harder'. But, like everyone, I find myself trying to keep going that little bit longer than necessary on a task, or agreeing to squeeze in an extra meeting.

On the other hand, I don't see anything wrong in enjoying material gains. My ambition is to be a millionaire in my own right – and I will be. We're sometimes taught that it's wrong to enjoy wealth. I don't know whether that's our British modesty or something else, but I don't see anything wrong with appreciating the good things of life. As long as you're prepared to work hard, then it's to be encouraged. But again it's all down to balance. Materialism is shallow and short-lived and, in the end, unreal. There's no point in having a dockside penthouse, a fridge full of champagne and a wardrobe full of Gucci clothes if you've no one to share it with.

The Apprentice was a great stepping stone in my life, taking me onto a new path towards new opportunities. The public recognition of my abilities helped me to sweep away any remaining doubts I had once and for all and become a more confident, mature person. I believe that I won, not because of what I did for the cameras, but because of the kind of person I am. I think my great strength is being able to sit back and listen. I hear what is being said and I analyse what is required of a situation. I exercise detachment – I don't jump in with both feet, shouting the odds about the first thing that comes into my head. I give a relevant, considered, unemotional answer, rather than wasting my energy in useless conflict and debate. That's my style – and *The Apprentice* has helped me define it publicly.

I realise that my experience is one that is unlikely to be repeated in the lives of many people. But you don't have to have been on *The Apprentice* to learn the lessons it has to teach. The thought I would like to leave you with is that all of us can create our own success, provided that we know what that success looks like to us, and acknowledge that for every person it's different. We can all recognise our strengths and act on them. Equally, all of us can acknowledge our weaknesses and get people on board who can provide the skills we are lacking. Don't sit around thinking that others are much better equipped to deal with a situation than you – the odds are they're thinking the same about you. Believe in yourself and go for what you want to achieve.

You might be unhappy because you're stuck in a job you

find boring, or frustrated because you haven't got the right paper qualifications to do what you want to do. It might seem as though there's no way out, but take a moment to think about my story. I've proved that it's possible to change your own future. I wasn't born with a silver spoon in my mouth and I didn't pass through school with flying colours. Yet I was able to change the path of my life one step at a time. You can do it too!

It's simple, but that first step I always talk about is vital. If you're unhappy in your current career, design a new CV and start sending it out. Fill in that application form that's gathering dust on your table. No one will know how talented you are if you don't tell them. Don't take no for an answer. Keep trying. Keep re-evaluating yourself and your aims. Believe in yourself. You can do it! Success has never just dropped into my lap – I've had to work hard, recognise my strengths and create my own opportunities. It's not easy, but if you believe in yourself, you can achieve the success you dream of.

I know I'm not alone in having had difficult elements in my life. There are thousands – hundreds of thousands – who have had a worse time than me. I've chosen to talk about it because I want people to understand that they don't have to be held back by their past. You can't change it, but you can build on it and use it to change the future. There is a popular saying that 'biography is just your story, not your destiny' and I truly believe that. The responsibility for the path your life takes is ultimately in your own hands. I may have had some rough patches – but I don't see myself as a victim. I'm not 'poor Michelle' – I'm a successful businesswoman who just happens to have had to overcome some tough obstacles. The good in my life now far outweighs the bad, because I refused to let the negative things plough me under.

I look back on last year and can't believe how much it has contained. Some of those moments have been exhilarating, others debilitating. However, I can honestly say that I am grateful for most of the experiences in my life because they have taught me so much about myself and made me a more rounded and stronger person. I like to see the positives and learn from everything that happens to me. This year has certainly given me a whole host of new lessons. I feel very positive and excited about what the future holds for me.

I often think of a speech made by Steve Jobs, the CEO of Apple and Pixar. He says that when you go through life, things happen to you and you don't understand why, but you just have to keep faith. It's only when you get further on in life that you can look back and see how the dots have joined up. I think that's how my life has been. I believe that there's a reason why I went on *The Apprentice*, why I won it, got pregnant, lost the baby. I think there are reasons for all of that which have yet to become clear, just as the effects of the distant past are now becoming clear in my mind.

CHAPTER TWENTY-FOUR

Pain is Temporary, Failure is For Ever

When I first decided to share my story in this book, my main hope was that someone, somewhere would read it and find it inspiring enough to change their life for the better. My journey from the worst moments of my past to a successful career in business and in the media is surely proof that anything is indeed possible. If one or two people could, in the pages of my book, find enough self-belief to move on and achieve their dreams, then I felt I would have achieved something truly worthwhile. As it turned out, I was totally unprepared for the tidal wave of response I received from readers of the hardback edition. So many people have contacted me, or posted reviews saying that they have been inspired to go for their goals and to understand that they can now make things happen for themselves. One of the greatest pleasures in the past year has been reading these comments and sharing the exhilaration of others who feel empowered to go on and reach their full potential.

With this in mind, I've decided that it's important to share some of the significant things that have happened to me since I first wrote *Anything is Possible*. My life over the last year has been a speeding whirlwind, some of it great, some of it truly soul destroying. Some days I've leapt excitedly out of bed and others I have hidden myself firmly under the covers, hoping the duvet would somehow swallow me up! For me, reality TV has been a strange thing. It plucked me from the obscurity of being 'normal' and put me on a nationwide platform available to scrutiny, criticism and expectation. I was never offered support through the process and at times it has been hard to cope with the pressure and to know how to deal with and respond to it appropriately. An occasion that springs to mind was soon after the loss of my baby when I told a broadsheet reporter to leave my home after he continuously put inappropriate questions to me that were firmly outside the remit of our agreed interview. He didn't take it to well and needless to say his article about me was, shall we say, less then favourable. After I lost the baby, I hit rock bottom and tried hard to pull myself together but it was really tough. As I mentioned earlier in the book, Scissorhands was an amazing thing for me; it gave me discipline, focus and confidence at a time when I needed it most.

The whole *Apprentice* experience, getting pregnant and then losing my baby has made me deeply question what it is I truly want from my life. I've always focused 100 per cent on my career and never given much thought or focus to anything else. Then all of a sudden, I found myself pregnant and, as I've described, the mixed feelings I experienced were incredible. All of a sudden I had something else in my life that was not related to business, career, materialism, etc., and it was overwhelming.

Since losing my baby, I have spent a large amount of time focusing on myself and trying to work out what my true purpose and passions are in life. I've done a lot of self-development work, read hundreds of inspirational books and attended lots of seminars and workshops. I've taken several breaks away to allow me to see things clearly and work out what it is I truly want. It's been a difficult journey because I have really had to analyse myself and admit to my weaknesses, which can be very painful, but I firmly believe that if we don't know what it is that we truly want, we don't have a chance of finding it. Look at it this way: if we set off in our car with no idea of where we were going, how on earth would we know which direction to travel in and when to celebrate arriving at the destination? I believe life is like that. We have to know what makes us happy and what we are striving for. We have to understand our purpose and what it is we truly value and believe in. Until we know this, I don't believe we can find true happiness; after all, success without fulfilment is nothing short of failure in disguise.

While Time hasn't stood still for me over the last year, it has allowed me to continue to grow and develop and to learn from the lessons and opportunities life has brought. As I've mentioned, it hasn't all been easy, but then I wouldn't expect it to be. Anything that's worthwhile has to be grafted for with all the strength and determination you have at your disposal. It's no good sitting there with your head in your hands thinking 'Why Me?' and I've had the sharpest possible reminder of this recently, when I had to face every woman's nightmare – a cervical cancer scare. It came at the worst possible time for me, as I was preparing to raise money for charity by running my first ever London Marathon. I'm going to share with you how my attitude of mind over matter got me through both the marathon and my medical treatment, using what has now become one of my mantras, 'Pain is temporary, failure is for ever'.

It was a bit of an impulsive decision for me to enter the marathon, coming as I was from a position of no great athletic fitness or robust health. A lot of people out there are probably overwhelmed by the thought of attempting a marathon – and to be honest, I was one of them. When I committed to doing it, I was very excited, particularly at the thought of raising money for the NSPCC and Well Child, which were my chosen charities. But when I put my trainers on for the first time I remembered just how boring I found running and how much I hated it. And I was going to have to do it for twenty-six and a half miles, in front of everybody. The media were watching, waiting for me to fail, and there was no way on this planet I was going to back out and let them call me a quitter. I embarked on my training plan, deciding to ease myself in gently and go for a run once round Clapham Common. I kept going for about five minutes and thought I was going to pass out! I ended up laid out in a star shape on the ground, wondering if I was going to die. I was out of breath, sweating, couldn't talk, couldn't move. I kept thinking, 'Oh my God, this is just one horrific nightmare.' The second time started off better. I set off round the common, managed to keep going and jog all the way home, then discovered I had somehow lost my house keys during my run. I was locked out with no way of getting back in, no phone, no money – nothing, just me and my running gear. I had to go round the whole common a second time to try and find the keys (which I couldn't!). I ended up sitting on my own doorstep for two and a half hours till one of the neighbours came home. I then rang a locksmith who had to change my locks. I learned two lessons that day. One: always take a phone and some money with you when you go out running, just in case. And two: next time you shut yourself out go and get them to pick the locks of some luxury penthouse in Kensington where you'd really like to live. The locksmith never once asked for my ID!

It was after training session four that I really thought someone might be trying to tell me something. I was running along the South Bank in London when my knee gave way beneath me. The pain was terrible. I was crying, unable to move, not knowing what to do next. It was a low point and I started thinking, 'I can't do this, how am I going to get out of it?' Then I remembered. No one was going to get a chance to write headlines about 'Michelle "Quitter" Dewberry'. I thought about the charities I was representing. I thought about how much I wanted to succeed. Then I gave myself a good talking to. 'You're not going to fail at this hurdle, Michelle. It's pathetic to think of quitting. You're going to run this marathon and nothing's going to stop you.' I consulted a physiotherapist, who told me I'd injured the cartilage and had to have six weeks' treatment before I could run again. That was a major blow. It was well into January by now and the marathon was in April. It was going to seriously disrupt any sensible training programme.

I rested the knee and started taking a glucosamine supplement, which is supposed to help joint suppleness. It seemed to do the trick for me. In March I was able to do a couple of six-mile runs. Unfortunately we were by now just about three weeks away from the marathon and I was feeling like death after six miles, unable to comprehend the idea of another twenty on top of that. I was beginning to feel seriously worried. On impulse, I decided the best thing would be to run a half marathon at the weekend. I Googled 'half marathons' and found that there was only one I could do between then and the London Marathon and that was in Reading, the following day! I contacted the organisers, who kindly let me enter, with a friend, at this incredibly short notice.

I borrowed a pacing watch and decided to do the race one mile at a time. I'd look at the watch and say to myself, 'I've got point eight of a mile to go . . . point six . . . point four . . . Yes! I've done my mile!' over and over again. When I got to twelve miles, I said to myself, 'Right, you've got to use every ounce of juice in your body and aim for a sprint finish.' However, because I'd been focusing so strongly on the watch, I had no real conception of how long a mile was in running terms, so I was sprinting far too early. My running partner was wondering what on earth I was doing, upping the pace so early, but I kept running and running, thinking, 'Where's the finishing line? Where's the finishing line?' I sprinted into the Madejski stadium in Reading feeling like I was going to die. I saw the advertising boards, ran straight at them and threw up. It was horrible. Not an attractive finish. But we did it in one hour and fifty-four minutes, which was an outstanding achievement.

I went out for a final distance run of seventeen and a half miles with a personal trainer – well, I use the word 'run' lightly.

I did most of it at a 'Dad' run as Peter Kay calls it – you move your arms and look like you're running, but you're not going at much more than walking pace. I did that for seven miles then walked the remaining ten. It was absolute agony. I kept trying to start running again, but couldn't because I'd slowed to a walk and it was impossible to increase the pace again. The marathon was getting closer and closer and things were not looking good. It was at this point, two weeks before the big day, that my cancer scare began in earnest.

I'd had an abnormal smear test in January – something that had happened before – and been called back for a colposcopy. That's where they examine the cervix and surrounding area to look for any abnormalities. It's not particularly pleasant, and it wasn't helped by the fact that as I lay on the couch, naked from the waist down with my legs in stirrups, the doctor came into the room and said, 'Oh my God, it's Michelle off *The Apprentice*!' I promise you I would have preferred not to have anyone know who I was at that moment – I was mortified! Anyway, she did the test and realised that the patch of abnormal cells was much worse than they'd thought it would be. They wanted to operate on me there and then, but it would have put an end to any hope of running in the marathon. I insisted that the operation would have to wait until afterwards, so they agreed to do a 'tissue grab', where they remove a portion of the cervix to send off for analysis.

I was devastated by the thought that I might have cervical cancer. I kept thinking, 'Why do these problems keep happening to me?' I'd gone through the problems of endometriosis, which meant that it would be much harder for me to have children; I was still suffering a severe emotional reaction to the loss of my baby a few months earlier; now the chances were that I had cancer cells present. It didn't seem fair. Part of me wanted to give in: have the operation, withdraw from the race and hope that people would understand. But some stubborn part of me refused to give up hope. Besides, I knew from experience how cruel the media can be. They'd say it was an excuse, try to write me off as a failure. I wasn't going to let them do it.

The weekend before the race I managed to find a really good running club called Clapham Chasers. I went along and did a ten mile run. I met a lovely girl there called Nicola, who's become a great friend. She was planning her week, running every single day. Fifteen miles one day, then slow it down to eleven, ten, down to three. She was asking what I intended to do and I muttered, 'I'm just going to take things easy for the last week.' I didn't do a thing. I rested instead, making sure I had no late nights and no alcohol. Four days before the race I started carb-loading. I had nothing to eat but carbohydrate. For breakfast I'd have porridge and toast. For lunch, jacket potato. For dinner, pasta and bread. Pasta and bread! Who eats pasta and bread? I drank four litres of water every single day, to get my body in a good state. The day before, I ran to the end of my street and back. It nearly killed me. I was thinking, 'My God, what have I let myself in for?'

On the day of the marathon, I was absolutely crapping myself with terror. I had to meet the other 'celebrity' competitors at 6 a.m. so we could all get a bus down to the start. The race didn't start till ten, but I had to get up at five! I was miserable about the early start, worried about the race, wondering how it would take a toll on my body and suffering from a sleepless night. Once we got down to the start, though, it was very exciting. Everyone seemed to know what they were doing, taping their toes together, putting Vaseline over their feet, preparing in various ways. I decided my strategy would be to eat. I had lots of energy bars and porridge. Gordon Ramsay was there with his wife and they were absolutely lovely. Matt Dawson was there with his girlfriend and we really got along well. I started chatting to people and really looking forward to it. Someone told me to put Vaseline on my feet, so I did. And before I knew it, it was time to go.

All I remember from the start is this absolute stampede. Everyone seemed to be pushing and shoving. Celebrities get put in the front row, because of the photo opportunity, but that meant the elite runners were immediately behind us. What they're worried about is their time. How I managed to survive that first half-mile is beyond me. I was dad-running while all these international athletes thundered past in a stampede. I remember we passed a speed camera and I called out to one of the other runners, 'We'd better slow down – we don't want to get done!' but he didn't find me amusing in the slightest. I thought, 'God, this is going to be hard work,' but decided I was just going to enjoy the experience. I had no real comprehension of time passing and stopped several times to visit the loo or fasten my shoes, etc.

Then we got on to the stage where there were spectators watching and suddenly it started to become fun. I was dancing down the street to 'Amarillo', doing the YMCA, high-fiving all the children and it was actually very pleasant. It was sweltering hot – the hottest London Marathon yet at 27°C – but I didn't even notice. I started to get my head together. I said to myself, 'Right, Michelle. At Mile Two we're going to imagine the *Daily Mirror*'s there, waiting to write about you failing. At Mile Four it'll be the *News of the World*, and so on.' So as I ran I was ticking them off in my mind: 'I've passed the *Mirror*, so they can't say I've failed, I've passed the *News of the World* so they can't call me a quitter, etc., etc. When you register, you get pace bands which help you run to the time you're aiming for. My mate Nicola had got a band for three and a half hours, but I had no idea what I was going to do. So I had a selection of pace bands for six and a half hours, six, five and a half and five hours. Everyone thought it was hilarious that I was wearing these all the way up my arm! As I'd been using my imaginary newspaper reporters to keep me going, I didn't really look at the pace bands until about Mile Ten, when I thought I'd better have a look and see how I was doing. I couldn't believe it. I was well ahead of the first three and not far off the five hour target. Not having done a marathon before I was thinking, 'What do I do now? Shall I try to pace myself to this, or what?' I realised once again that I hadn't prepared myself properly in the way that most of the runners had. In the end, I just kept on going and trying to enjoy it.

When I got to Mile Seventeen I just saw this massive banner saying *Michelle Dewberry, Anything is Possible*, and there were my family, all cheering. It was a fantastic moment and really encouraged me. Each time I saw my friends along the route I'd dance around and high-five them – it gave me such a boost. It was all going really well until, at Mile Twenty, the trouble started.

I thought I had a stone in my shoe. I was flicking my foot to try to dislodge it, so that I wouldn't have to stop, but it wouldn't come out. I decided the only thing for it was to pull over to the railings and take my shoe off. The spectators recognised me from *The Apprentice* and were cheering and patting my back. Then, as I peeled my sock off they stopped. Someone said, 'Oh my God, look at your foot.' I was looking. The toes on my right foot had swollen so they appeared to have merged into one. They were blistered and bleeding and yellow. The main part of the foot had turned blue. Seeing them, I realised how much pain I was in.

I kept thinking, 'What shall I do, what shall I do?' Should I go to St John Ambulance, the first-aid post, and get them treated? The left foot was obviously going to be in the same state, surely I couldn't continue with them like this? Then I thought of the distance I'd completed. If I stopped now for treatment I knew I'd never get started again. I knew I had to somehow put my shoe back on the mess that was my right foot – and run for the finish line.

It was really painful. I kept saying to myself, 'Pain is temporary, failure is for ever. My feet will get back to normal in six months or so, but how will I feel about myself if I've dropped out?' I was also battling severe nausea – a sick feeling that I've never experienced the like of in my life. I'd been eating jelly babies all the way around the course to give me energy and had obviously eaten way too many! I zoned myself into a world where nothing existed but two mantras: *pain is temporary, failure is for ever* and *don't stop, don't stop*.

I made it to the final mile and wondered if I should try a

sprint finish. Then I decided not to push it. A fellow runner had passed out a few metres in front of me and I knew I didn't want that to happen to me. I'd seen someone being given oxygen on Mile Six and I knew that I was already pushing myself beyond my limits. What I was doing was no easy task. So I did it at a dad-run, crossed the line and threw my arms in the air. I'd completed the marathon in *four hours and thirty-three minutes*! Unbelievable! My first thought was, 'If I can do this, what am I capable of if I actually train hard? Next year I'm going to see what my body can do if I push it.'

On the finishing line I did an interview with the BBC. Then I got carted off to St John in a wheelchair. They told me I'd had the wrong socks on and laced my shoes too tight, cutting down the circulation to my feet. They warned I was going to lose my toenails, and they were right. All but two fell off in the following weeks. My feet were agony and I had to walk in slippers for days afterwards. But when I went to the grandstand to find my family, all the pain receded. They'd put up huge posters, my mum was dancing and waving her arms around, on a natural high, saying 'That's my daughter' to anyone who'd listen. We celebrated for a bit and cheered on anyone who was struggling towards the finishing line, yelling 'Come on! You can do it!' over and over again. Adidas gave me a T-shirt with a great slogan on it. It says, *You saw the impossible. I saw the finishing line.* That for me is so true. The marathon taught me that your mind is the most powerful tool you have been blessed with and with the right attitude you can overcome anything. My feet were bleeding, swollen, cut and blue, but I finished. I've been on nights out when my shoes have given me a little blister and

I've had to go home because I've felt I can't get on the dance floor. But if you'd seen my feet during the race . . . well, there was no comparison. What kept me going was the knowledge that if I stopped, my dream was over. The dream was more important than the temporary pain. It was without doubt one of the best things I've ever done in my life and one of the proudest moments of my life. Only one per cent of the population will run a marathon. And I'm one of them!

Once the marathon was over, I had to find the strength to deal with my cancer scare. When I went back, the results weren't encouraging. The tissue grab had confirmed that there was a large section of abnormal cells. I had to have an operation. They removed the affected area of my cervix. I was devastated. I was convinced that I wouldn't be able to have children. All the feelings of loss I'd experienced when I miscarried my baby were intensified. I'm still struggling to come to terms with that on a daily basis and to find that I was once again having to have surgery made my prospects of motherhood seem even more unlikely. I went through moments of complete despair. Endometriosis, miscarriage, cervical cancer – these are all things that women may have to face in their lives; why did I have to have every single one of them? It really upset me. Eventually I had a letter to say that all the cancerous cells had been removed and I was on six-month check-ups. It felt like a major reprieve.

Once the operation was over, I started to recover emotionally.

I combined a work trip to Egypt with a short break to relax. I took a massive stack of books and read the stories of people like Branson and Murdoch, all of whom I find massively inspirational. I was away on this trip when the final of *The Apprentice* Series Three occurred. It gave me a great sense of perspective. When I'd won the show, it felt like it was the most important thing in everyone's lives. Being away from the UK at the same time the following year showed me that was not the case. It was very grounding. In the year after the show I'd felt like I was being swept along by a river and that somehow my life was not in my own hands. It felt strange; I was always used to being in control of my own destiny but for a period of time it felt as if I had no control. But now I knew I was managing to seize back the control and make my own decisions about the way I want my life to be.

I mentioned earlier that I have done a lot of self-reflection over the last year and have worked hard to understand what it is I truly want. I have defined my purpose as being 'To achieve significant success and to help others to do the same by guiding, mentoring and coaching them. I will also be in a financial position that allows me to treat myself, friends, family and charities.'

Since *The Apprentice,* I've taken on numerous speaking engagements on the theme of 'Anything is Possible'. I've spoken at corporate events, worked with people in care and have sessions lined up to help with rehabilitating prisoners. I also run 'Anything is Possible' workshops where I teach people that they can be anything they want to be. My message is always: work out what it is you want, get the right mindset, then go hell for leather towards achieving it. Ignore the dream-stealers

– people who laugh at your ideas – and don't let them win. I've realised that my true passion is helping others to achieve their potential and have decided to establish a company that expands on my Anything is Possible brand and offers a range of seminars, workshops and coaching to people, ranging from business through to motivational and interpersonal skills.

I've also done several TV appearances since *The Apprentice*, including *This Week* and *The Daily Politics Show* with Andrew Neill, where I talked about the need to help people off benefits and encourage them to empower themselves and get back to work by building up their confidence and motivation. Lord Strathclyde was there from the Conservative party and said I was unbelievable! He suggested I should become an MP for his party. I also had quite a few emails from viewers saying I should go into politics. I'm attracted by the difference that you can make as an MP, but I think it's something I might consider a few years down the line, rather than now. Never say never, eh!

I enjoy the TV work and would love to expand into sensible, topical areas. I was invited to present an architecture programme for BBC1, called *Building Britain*. It looked at how Hull has been regenerated and considered its past and its future. We studied the changes that building and design create in an area and how they are affecting local people and the community. It was great to go back to my home town and study it in this way. Originally the producer had intended to get an actress in to record the voiceovers, but I asked if I could have a go at it. They were really impressed with the result and decided to keep my voice on it. That was great.

I was at a reception in Downing Street when Jo Elvin, the editor of *Glamour* magazine, and I got chatting. She suggested I might like to do something with them. I told her that I like to inspire other people and help them make positive changes in their lives, so we came up with an idea for a competition. The three winning readers will get me as a life coach for six months. I'll work with them to help them define and achieve their goals. *Glamour* is the UK's biggest circulating glossy magazine, so it's going to be great. That particular reception was part of my work with Women's Aid, a charity that helps victims of domestic violence. I've also been supporting an initiative to gain recognition for the problems that women suffer with endometriosis. There's a very talented photographer called Klarke Caplin who also has the condition and she's put together a fantastic calendar to promote awareness. The theme was Hitchcock films – next year it's going to be Moulin Rouge and I'm already booked in for a shoot. I've also done work for other charities, helping families get their finances back on track and campaigning to get women greater opportunities on the business ladder. Next year I'm going to focus on my two chosen charities, the NSPCC and The Prince's Trust, and really concentrate on giving them my all. I have decided to focus on physical challenges and have lined up a place in the London Triathlon (run, swim and cycle) as well as doing the marathon, and I am also completing a 1000-mile cycle ride from Nice to London! I love new challenges and I hope that the charities will benefit tremendously from my efforts. What I want is to have a really outstanding life. I don't want to settle for a pleasant or easy life – I want to make a difference and to help other people to do the same.

I've come to a realisation over the past months that I don't have to define myself and keep myself shut in one particular compartment. I used to struggle to categorise myself. Now I've accepted that I can be a multitude of things and have a multitude of interests. When the whole celebrity thing started, it used to really worry me. People were trying to categorise me and define who Michelle was, when I didn't really know myself. The media struggled to put me into a box. I was The Blonde Pretty One, but I was also The Driven Businesswoman. It used to worry me, but now I am confident enough to admit that I am a lot of things. I can go on to *Big Brother's Big Mouth* and talk about reality TV, but equally I can go onto the *Politics Show* and talk about things that have real substance. I can be equally at home in either of those environments and that's something to be proud of, not something to worry about.

Viewers watch celebrity shows like *The Apprentice* and dream of the instant fame, but it's not always the way people perceive it to be. In some ways it prevents you from living a normal life, because everybody knows who you are and everyone wants a piece of you. British society has this amazing ability to put someone high on a pedestal then turn round and whack them off it again. People see the nice side of celebrity life, the parties and the glamour. Of course it's enjoyable, of course it's good fun. There are some great moments. But it can also be a weird and confusing lifestyle. If you go on to shows or do interviews where people are interested in you, it's very easy to allow your ego to become inflated, because the spotlight is turned your way. If you do get into the media and suddenly have a profile, the best piece of advice I can offer is to have a 'plan B'. Media work should only ever be a 'nice to have' rather than a desperate need. Once you become desperate for it, you can bet your bottom dollar you will be setting yourself up for a whole lot of heartache! I have a successful consultancy (Michelle Dewberry Ltd) and a whole other host of business interests and investments, and that is what keeps me sane.

Overall, the past year has been (and I hate to be cheesy) a rollercoaster. I have had a lot of turmoil and a loss of privacy but ultimately I have learnt so much about myself, made some great friends and done some great work supporting charity initiatives. All of which I am truly greatful for.

As I mentioned earlier, to achieve success in life, you have to know what success means to you. Once you do, the sky is the limit.

I wish you well in your endeavours and please do check out my website www.michelledewberry.com to see how I can help you, or simply to give me feedback on my book. I would love to hear from you.

With love and very best wishes always,

Michelle x

Conclusion

Now that I've told you my story, you can see how I've dealt with some of the situations that have cropped up in my life. I hope that sharing my experiences has been helpful, particularly to anyone who feels they're at a crossroads in their lives. Most people at some time or another want to change direction in their career or their personal life and if my story has inspired just one person to turn their life around, I will be over the moon. I feel I've learned a lot of lessons along the way about making the most of myself. So I'd like to share the top ten of them with you now and hopefully they will be of use to you in taking that first step towards the future you want for yourself. I've tailored the tips below to your career, but they can be adapted across many different scenarios beyond work.

1 Decide what you want from life

Before you can make any changes, you have to decide what you want from life. You need to be sure to think about what *you* want, not what your family, friends and employers want you to do. Identify your long-term goals. They may appear dauntingly far from your present position – but don't worry about that. Life's journeys can't be completed in a single day. Plan your route carefully and you will get where you want to be in the end. Write down a career plan. What job do you dream of doing in, say, five years' time? What experience will you need? Are there any paper qualifications which would help you? Now, decide on the steps you are going to take to achieve your goal.

It's very important to commit your thoughts to paper, so that they are a permanent record of your determination. Not only will this help spur you on to meet your deadlines, it will also be a record that will help you look back with pride on how far you have come. Is there a position that will help you gain the experience you need and help you achieve your ultimate aim? Visualise yourself in that job and write down a realistic date by which you hope to have got it. Remember, you may need to take a drop in salary or working conditions to get it; but don't let that put you off. It is the first step on your journey and if you don't take it, you will never get to the place you want to be. Getting what you want out of life demands sacrifices. You may be comfortable where you are, but are you happy? Probably not, if you are hankering after something else.

I chose to take a drop in salary when I took that YTS place with St John Ambulance and it was certainly worth it for me. I looked on it as an investment in my future. It enabled me to move from 'jobs' in retail to 'a career' in office work, and it was one of the turning points of my life. It was a move into an environment where I could allow my own particular skills to develop and equip myself for the future that I wanted. That, in my view, amply compensated for any shortfall in earnings. If you decide the end is not worth the means and you are not prepared to make short-term sacrifices, then fair enough. But if that is the case you must strike a bargain with yourself to stop thinking negative, dissatisfied thoughts. Staying where you are has to be a positive step too – and you can look for growth in your personal life or challenges in your out-of-work interests. But you will see what you want more clearly once you have worked out your career/life plan and written it down.

Another important element to consider is how to get the training you need to progress. Once again, this may require short-term investment of time and money – but again, it is important to weigh this against the future benefits. As I'm always saying, just because you didn't do well at school, it doesn't mean you have to write yourself off. There are plenty of second chances nowadays for people to qualify outside the standard school and college system. Look on the Internet and find out what courses are available. Or ask advice at your library, Jobcentre or advisory organisations like Businesslink. It's simple, but it's that vital first step towards arming yourself for your new career.

You may have found, as I did, that studying at school didn't interest you very much. Don't let that put you off. Once you get started on something that you really want to do and that will be useful in attaining your goals, you may find that studying is a whole lot more interesting. Lots of us find it easier to work when we have a goal in sight. I took two NVQs, a typing course, IT exams, an HNC, a Project Management accreditation and then went on to take up an Open University course which I'm still following. I did all of this in my own time and at my own expense. And I can categorically say that I've enjoyed those studies a lot more than I did my schoolwork!

Here is an example of one of the plans that I wrote when I was twenty-three:

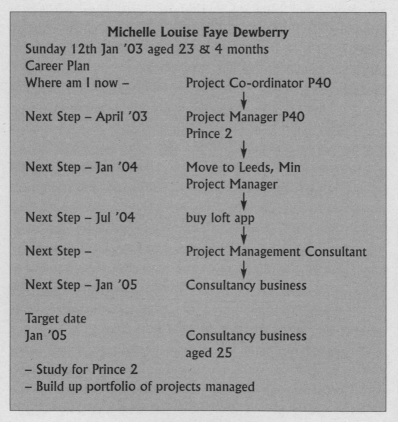

Michelle Louise Faye Dewberry
Sunday 12th Jan '03 aged 23 & 4 months
Career Plan

Where am I now –	Project Co-ordinator P40
Next Step – April '03	Project Manager P40 Prince 2
Next Step – Jan '04	Move to Leeds, Min Project Manager
Next Step – Jul '04	buy loft app
Next Step –	Project Management Consultant
Next Step – Jan '05	Consultancy business
Target date Jan '05	Consultancy business aged 25

– Study for Prince 2
– Build up portfolio of projects managed

2 Take the first step

Once you've got your career plan perfected and have sorted out which additional qualifications you need, don't make the mistake of sitting back and waiting for it all to drop into your lap. TAKE THAT ALL-IMPORTANT FIRST STEP! You must be pro-active – I can't stress that strongly enough. You may be talented, but no one's going to know that if you don't go out there and tell them, are they? You'll have pinpointed which companies you would like to work for and which firms offer the kind of jobs you want. Don't hang around wishing they'd advertise the post you want – approach them first. Ask which employment agencies they use for their recruiting; then get on their books. Keep trying. If you get a rejection letter – if you get ten – so what? Every 'no' you get takes you closer to the 'yes' you are about to receive.

Be determined. Keep believing in yourself and sooner or later you'll find people will start believing in you. I'm not saying it's easy. Believe me, there have been many times when I have tried to achieve something and have had so many people saying no to me that it can be difficult to keep going sometimes. But you have to; things won't happen for you if you give up. Maybe they haven't got a vacancy just yet for the post you've set your heart on but it's worth considering other offers. When I applied to Kingston Communications, they turned me down as a manager, but my application impressed them enough for them to offer me an alternative position. I took it, because I could see it was another step forward – a way in to the company I wanted to work for. I believe in seizing the opportunities that come your way – it's important not to let pride blind you to the alternatives that may be available.

3 Sell yourself

Your CV and application form are all-important. My primary advice to you here is to be yourself. Present your strengths honestly and concisely, and make sure you supply all the information that's asked for on the form or in the job advert. Be relevant. Don't try to be all things to all people – stick to expressing what and who you really are. You don't have to try to be funny. The application form for *The Apprentice* was the longest I've ever filled in, but I resisted the temptation to play it anything but straight. They wanted to know who I was and what I was like – it was up to me to show them.

Plan your answers in rough first, before you write them on the form and try to go through them with an objective eye, reading them as an employer would for the first time. Perhaps you could ask a friend to look through it with you and give you an honest opinion. I'm often asked to help my friends and family with their CVs. If you know someone who's in a position where they have to filter applications and interview people, don't be afraid to seek their advice. In the end, you must go with what you think is right, but it never hurts to listen to other people's opinions along the way.

Make sure you tell a prospective employer who you are and exactly why you are the right person for the job. What experience do you have? What use have you made of your strengths? In what way do your current achievements demonstrate your abilities? You might find this difficult, particularly if your paper qualifications don't quite fit – but don't worry. Energy, drive and the right attitude are all desirable qualities and there is scope for demonstrating them in any job. Even when I was working at Kwik Save I was showing my employability by merchandising and tidying during my spare time rather than sitting around waiting for customers. Look for the positive things you bring to your current job and tell your prospective employer about them. Otherwise how will he or she know how good you are?

Applications are your introduction to the employer and it can sometimes be hard to get them just right. When I was sixteen I wanted to work for Miss Selfridge. I approached them and asked how I could be sure of getting a job with them. They said I should write a letter. 'Fair enough,' I said. 'But you must get hundreds of letters. How do I make sure you pick me out of all the rest?' The manager said that I would just have to make it different from the others, so it got noticed. I went away and planned my letter and wrote it on fluorescent pink paper, and posted it in a matching fluorescent pink envelope. And guess what? I never heard back from them! I guess that wasn't the sort of 'different' that they wanted.

My application to Kingston Communications was more successful, although by that time I'd abandoned the bright pink paper for a classy, marble effect card, which seemed to go down better. I used it to prepare a presentation for the interview, which I'm still quite proud of to this day. I'd pre-empted all the questions I thought they were likely to ask me, and written the answers out clearly in bullet points, distributing copies to everyone in the room. Of course that might not be appropriate in every situation, but it's important to find an approach that will make you stand out – in a good way – from the other candidates.

4 Do your research

When you are offered an interview, it's important to maximise your opportunity by doing as much preparation work as you can, so that you can be sure of making the right impression. Google can be an important tool here – it's so easy to do an Internet search and find out as much as possible about your prospective employers. If they have a company website, study it – you'll be able to learn plenty about how they wish to be perceived. Are there any stories in the news about them? You can find out if they are planning any new acquisitions, for example, or study their particular branding.

Before the day of the interview, make sure you know how to get there and how long your journey will take. Whatever your attitude to punctuality in general, it's not good to be late for a job interview. Make sure you dress appropriately. You can do some research first and find out what best fits their corporate image. One of my mates rang me up recently and asked about what to wear to an interview with a PR company. I suggested she hung around outside the offices of the company she was interested in (discreetly of course, I didn't want her being carted away by the police for being a stalker), just to see how their current employees dressed. Was it ultra fashionable or casual? Or conservative? Once she'd got a feel for what the staff were wearing it was easier to make a judgement on what look she should go for.

On the day, your advance research should give you some idea of the kind of questions you'll be asked. Give plenty of thought to this. You've looked up the field they operate in; focus on the way the job you're applying for is going to fit in to this overall picture. Try to have some answers ready – but don't end up sounding too rehearsed. Be clear and concise in what you have to say, and make sure that you answer the question you're being asked, rather than the one you thought they would throw at you. That means listening to what the people interviewing are saying. It's a good idea to be prepared for the more general questions that employers often throw at you. For example, one favourite seems to be 'You've identified your strengths – what do you perceive as your weaknesses?' It's easy to be lured into the trap of sounding negative about yourself on this one, but my advice to you is to turn it round and use it as another opportunity to demonstrate the positive.

'Yes, I'm better at doing X than at doing Y, but because I

recognise it I am currently doing/planning to do this about it.' This sort of answer can turn your admission of a weakness round and gives you the opportunity to bring in something you want to do, such as further training or going to night school. Better still is an answer that acknowledges a weakness, but presents it as a pointer to an underlying strength. For example, I might give the following answer: 'I do acknowledge that I can be impatient with others who aren't showing my level of commitment to a project. In the past this may have led to me being frustrated but now I take time to understand the team a lot more at the start of the project and set goals and timeframes upfront.'

This answer accepts that I'm not perfect and am willing to take steps to meet others half way – but I'm also using the opportun- -ity to stress one of my strengths – my dedication and hard work.

Whatever answer you give has to ring true. It's no good pre- tending to be something you're not. You have to be yourself. If they point out a weakness in you as a candidate – for example a lack of experience in your chosen field – acknowledge it, but use the technique I've outlined above to turn it round and explain what you plan to do about it. Present yourself confidently, but don't fall into the trap of appearing arrogant. It's easy to allow nerves to get the better of you, but try to stay calm. In the inter- views for *The Apprentice*, so many people seemed to have a lot to say for themselves, most of which, I think, was due to pressure. Because I was determined to be myself, I think I was able to act more naturally and react more clearly to what was being said. I didn't fall into the trap of sounding off about how brilliant I was; I let my actions speak for themselves.

An interview doesn't have to be a one-way process. It's your chance to find out about the company too, its ambitions, culture and current projects. You need to decide whether it's the right place for you to work. I like to ask interviewers about their policy for investing in people and how they plan to invest in my career, should I be given the job. There's no harm in letting a prospective employer know that you are ambitious and want to progress within the company. Asking this kind of question can lead them naturally on to a discussion about how your career could develop within the firm and what additional training might be on offer. I also find it helpful to ask what interested them in my application – what made them choose to interview me? There's no harm in getting them to define why they chose you. It's a good opportunity to get some feedback about yourself that will help you pinpoint your own strengths.

If you've done your homework, you'll be able to ask questions about the company, but do keep them relevant. For example, saying 'I see you're expanding – I notice you're in the process of acquiring shares in company X' just shows that you've done a bit of research. On the other hand, 'I see that you're in the process of acquiring shares in company X – what does that mean to the role we are discussing. Would there be any impact and does that mean I would also be involved in providing back-up for product Y?' has more of a point to it.

At the age of eighteen, when I walked into my interview with Kingston Communications and presented each person in the room with their folder, it was my way of taking control of the situation. By giving them my answers to the questions they were likely to ask, I was ensuring the points I wanted to put over were covered in the way I wanted them to be. It also meant that discussions could develop from the starting points I'd selected, rather than leaving the reins solely in the hands of my interviewers. I'm not saying that this technique would be the right one to use in every situation, but it's a good example of how to be proactive as an interviewee.

5 Create a good impression

Eventually, all the preparation and hard work will pay off, and you'll get your new job. Be sure to note down your achievements on your life plan and update your aims if necessary. It's possible that your new appointment will put a different slant on the training process or on your career path. But don't throw away the old version of your plan. Keep it, as I've kept mine. If nothing else, it will be an interesting reference point to look back on and see how far you've travelled.

When you start work at a new place, it's time to build on the good impression you created at the interview stage. Continue to dress appropriately – people will be looking at the new arrival and first impressions are important. Be prepared and have all the tools you are likely to need at hand: pens and a notebook are essential, so have your own at the ready. The chances are that everything will be provided, but you don't want to be rushing round trying to find the key to the stationery cupboard when you're supposed to be at a meeting. Make sure that you are polite, courteous and punctual; take as many notes as you can; and try to meet as many people as possible during your first few days. If you're introduced to a big group of people at one time, jot down their names. I find, if I'm sitting round a table, that sketching out a diagram of where everyone's sitting with notes on who's who really helps. Using people's names is a good way of demonstrating that you're part of the team.

My way is always to observe before I speak and that's another of my tips. Use the first days to gain a thorough understanding of your new workplace. Watch everything and everyone. How do people interact with each other? Who gets on with who? Who gains people's respect – and who doesn't? Why? What are they doing? Learn from what you see; there will be skills you can emulate and mistakes you will definitely wish to avoid. Try to take a step back – you don't want to be so eager to make a good impression that you jump in with both feet and set everyone against you from the start. Ask plenty of questions, but don't commit yourself before you are sure you know what you want to achieve and how you want to achieve it. If I'm asked a direct question, such as: 'What are your plans for the project?' I will say something like: 'At the moment I'm just on an information gathering exercise and once I've come to a full understanding of the way things work here I'll be able to make an informed decision, which will be in the next day or so.'

As time goes on, keep your ear to the ground and identify areas in which you can make an impact. Look beyond your immediate work station. Is there a staff and social club? Intranet? A company magazine? Getting involved over and above the call of duty will help to get you noticed by the right people. How can you broaden your scope of responsibility to help you progress in the way you want to? At St John Ambulance the new computer system offered me the opportunity. It would have been quite easy to sit back and think 'I'm only the YTS admin girl; it's none of my business', but I seized the chance of learning something and got myself noticed as an achiever. I was then able to take it one step further and devise a training session to share my knowledge. That's a good example of how to demonstrate your potential to your employer.

Again, at Kingston, I pushed hard to learn IT skills and eventually took the Microsoft Professional exam. I asked to be included in the meeting with Tiscali, so that I could understand the relationship with the client. There's no harm in asking – the worst that can happen is that you'll be told no. I believe in demonstrating to your employer that you are prepared to go the extra mile in order to progress to where you want to be. There is absolutely no point in sitting around getting bored because you haven't enough to occupy you in your own narrow job parameters. Identify what needs doing and go for it. Your persistence will be rewarded.

6 Set clear expectations

Results are ultimately what will get you noticed. I try to under promise and over deliver. It's much better to say that you can manage x, y and z by a certain date, then deliver it with a, b and c as a bonus, than to raise expectations too high and fail to live up to them. If you're in a team situation, don't try to do everything yourself – learn to delegate. When I'm project managing I know every single detail of what's going on in the project, but I don't try to do it all myself. I just make sure that everyone is doing their job properly, according to their strengths. Also, if something is going wrong, I flag it up at the first possible opportunity. If your budget's going into overspend, don't stick your head in the sand and imagine it will somehow be all right in the end – alert people right away to the fact there's not enough money in the pot. Either the budget can be increased to meet reasonable demands – or the expectations can be cut to meet the budget. Either way you'll have done the right thing. When I was at Xenon Green, I made sure that Sir Alan Sugar was aware of my doubts about the company's viability, so that we didn't launch a project that would fail to deliver. Which would Sir Alan prefer? A proper feasibility study that gave a realistic view of profitability – or a high-profile company that would show no profit a year down the line? There's no contest, is there?

7 Find solutions rather than problems

Another of my tips for success at work is to find solutions, rather than problems. This might sound easier said than done but, in fact, it's down to how you present things. If something isn't working, take a look at it and understand why. Then think of ways you can get around it. Once you've done that, you can go to your boss and say: 'X isn't working as well as it should be because of Y. But if we do A, B or C, we should be able to resolve it.' That's so much better than sitting around grumbling about the way things are. An employee who identifies ways of putting things right is much more likely to make a good impression than one who is constantly negative.

8 Don't let your comfort zone hold you back

Ultimately you may at some point want to progress from the role you are in, whether that's within the same company or a different one. The way that I recognise when it's time to move on is when I've stopped learning or if I'm starting to feel stagnant. If you're not careful, you can fall into a habit. You end up doing something just because it's convenient and comfortable. With change always comes a move out of your comfort zone and it becomes just that: uncomfortable. Don't let that feeling put you off. You have to live up to that cheesy line of 'feeling the fear and doing it anyway'. Making change isn't easy, but if you want to progress it's worth the discomfort. I persevered with my job at Stoke, even though I wasn't happy, because I knew it was broadening my horizons and preparing me for the next step. Then, when the time was right, I moved on to London. I keep harping back to it but that's because it's important: you mustn't lose sight of your goals. They will remind you why you are doing this and where you are trying to get to.

9 Maintain a good work-life balance

I am a great advocate for hard work, but however important your career is, you must never forget to maintain a proper work-life balance. It is the key thing to enable you to have a happy life. Lots of people think that they need to work all day every day in the office to be judged as a success. You really don't. I believe, when you are at work, you should manage your time to ensure that you can deliver all requirements during the working hours available to you. It's all about working smarter, not longer. I think at the end of the evening and on weekends, it is imperative to have time where you 'switch off'. When I first came to London, I used to have a Blackberry and I fell into the trap of it being my 'Crackberry'; I would have it with me twenty-four hours a day, and if I went for dinner it would be on the table so I could answer the emails as they came in.

I have finally realised now that one of the keys to being successful is to balance your life. If you have a fun and varied social life with plenty of rest and a great support network, you will be able to achieve some great things. People sometimes say (I know I used to) that they can't switch off or they don't have hobbies, but there are always things you can do to increase your work-life balance.

Personally, one of my favourite ways of unwinding is by spending time in flotation tanks, and spas, but everyone will have their own special way of pampering themselves. Giving yourself time out ensures your body and mind are both fresh and ready for the challenges ahead. Sure, there are exceptional times when you need to give work all your undivided attention. But not every week.

If you find yourself working long hours as a matter of course, try to step back a little. What is the worst thing that's going to happen if you don't log on to your laptop on Saturday? I'm not saying that you should ignore deadlines; I'm saying that you should learn to judge which are the really important targets so that you can concentrate your energy on those. Don't procrastinate, so that you leave yourself with everything to do at the last minute. Create the right conditions for yourself to work effectively. I sometimes tell myself that things will go away if I ignore them, but they don't. It's best to tackle the unappealing tasks right away and get them over with, rather than letting them escalate. The Open University course I'm following taught us how to differentiate between a difficulty and a mess. A difficulty is a single problem that can be tackled and overcome. A mess is a tangled web of difficulties that have been allowed to spiral out of control. Don't allow your difficulties to become messes! Tackle them one by one as they arise.

And finally …

10 Believe in yourself

You will always come across people or situations that will pull you down. Often those things are out of your control. What is not out of your control, however, is the way you react to them.

I've said many times in this book that it is easier for us to remember the bad things rather than the good, but ultimately you can find a positive from nearly any situation, if you choose to.

When something bad has happened to me, I always try to find the good and try to get a sense of perspective. This can often be difficult when the bad things are intense, such as when I lost my sister or my baby. But ultimately, you can always draw some positives, which from my examples are that at least I was blessed to have had my sister in my life or, at least I was blessed to experience the feeling of my own child growing inside me. While both those things were short-lived, some people never get those opportunities.

My advice is simple: know yourself, where you are heading, how you are going to get there and have the self-belief that you can achieve it. Surround yourself with people who can help or support you and put your minor setbacks into perspective. Take time to take stock of your achievements and don't forget to give yourself a pat on the back when it's deserved.

Whatever you dream of doing, I'd like to wish you every success with it – and I know you will achieve it. Especially if, above all else, you remember to believe in yourself, because if you do … anything is possible …

Good luck!

Michelle X

I can see myself now. Each Tuesday evening, after my session at the local Brownies, I try to press the doorbell of the NatWest bank in Hull. I can nearly reach it — but not quite. It's so frustrating. I stand on tip-toe, finger pointing upwards, my arm stretching as high as it can go. The stone wall scratches me through my uniform and I can feel my body aching with the effort. It's always a little too far for me, but one day soon I'll get there ... I can't wait to grow!